# HOW TO START
# A BUSINESS
# WITHOUT QUITTING
# YOUR JOB

## *The Moonlight Entrepreneur's Guide*

Philip Holland

Ten Speed Press
Berkeley, California

*Also by Philip Holland*
The Entrepreur's Guide

TEN SPEED PRESS
Post Office Box 7123
Berkeley, California    94707

Cover design by Fifth Street Design
Text design by Merry K. Obrecht. Typography by Publication Services Inc.,
Champaign, Illinois

Quotes from the *Handbook of Small Business Data: 1988* reprinted by
permission of the Office of Advocacy, U.S. Small Business Administration.

Quotes from Joe Paterno originally appeared in an advertising campaign
from Panhandle Eastern Corporation. Reprinted by permission of Joe
Paterno.

Quotes from Dr. Muhammed Jamal originally appeared in the *National
Enquirer* (n.d.). Reprinted by permission of Dr. Muhammed Jamal.

**Library of Congress Cataloging-in-Publication Data**

Holland, Philip (Philip Clark)
    How to start a business without quitting your job : the moonlight
entrepreneur's guide / Philip Holland.
        p.   cm.
    ISBN 0-89815-449-9
    1. Supplementary employment.   2. New business enterprises.
I. Title.
HD8036.H65   1992
658. 1'141–dc20                                                91-37672
                                                                   CIP

Printed in the United States of America
    2   3   4   5   –   96   95   94   93   92

*To Peggy, with love*

# CONTENTS

CONTENTS

# Introduction

Let's face it—most Americans don't have *quite* enough entrepreneurial drive to start a business. We depend on jobs, not on running businesses, for earning a living.

Yet many new immigrants look upon starting a business as the best or in many cases the only way to make a living. Some are not educated. Many can't speak English. They come to America from the Far East or the Near East—from all over the world—and they're starting tens of thousands of new businesses every year. You can see them at the self-service gas stations and convenience stores; they may run your video store or the snack counter where you buy a doughnut. And you can spot them on the freeways, in their expensive cars.

One reason that few Americans go into business is that we have a deep-rooted fear of failure. Free enterprise gives us the opportunity to go into business, but not the courage. We look upon going into business as an unacceptable crapshoot. Or we're afraid of losing our vacations, pension plans, and medical insurance. Our upbringing dictates that our duty is to find a job when we graduate from school. So we accept working as the conventional way to make a living.

In the past, American jobs did provide us with dependable pay envelopes and long-range security. Not anymore. Job security is now the crapshoot as American companies struggle for survival. Entire layers of management are carved away, increasingly less frequently with golden handshakes.

So the idea of going into business receives a great deal of lip service these days. Yet ten years ago we didn't know how to spell *entrepreneur,* let alone pronounce it. Now it's the buzzword of politicians and business journalists, so much so that mothers no longer want their daughters to marry doctors—they want them to marry entrepreneurs. If all that is said about our golden age for entrepreneurs were true, one would expect to find hordes of Americans opting for it.

Let me assure you that they are not. The metamorphic transformation from employee to entrepreneur is infrequently experienced in American life. Full-blown entrepreneurs are members of an exclusive fellowship that is infinitesimal in comparison with the multitudes who depend on their traditional jobs. The chasm is too frightening to hurdle. There's too much to lose.

But who says we are obliged to quit our jobs when we start a business? I once did, but only because at the time I didn't know any better. It was a matter of having more guts than brains. Let the world know that I wouldn't do it again. It was an imprudent leap into a swim-or-drown struggle. If I had possessed more savvy than guts, I would have started out as a moonlight entrepreneur.

You are going to learn here how to overcome this fear of going into business and how to have both a job and a business at the same time: to enjoy the best of both worlds. This book will detail the *why, how,* and *where.*

A real estate broker will tell us that "one good investment is worth a lifetime of toil." Your job—a lifetime of toil—will provide not only your income and fringe benefits but the capital for starting your new business as well. And with any luck the moonlight business may become the investment worth more than your wearisome years of employment.

# PART ONE ▼ WHY

Who needs to moonlight? Perhaps you do. Here are practical reasons why becoming a moonlight entrepreneur could become your ticket to financial security and also self-realization.

# CHAPTER ONE

# What Have You Got To ~~Lose~~ Gain?

T his book describes the *how to* of juggling a job and business, not the *why*. Yet it is worth taking a brief look into the benefits of business ownership. Your job provides income and fringes, but the moonlight business is going to become your "candy store."

Also, I don't want you to dwell too much on the risks of going into business without anticipating the rewards. You will be reminded enough about business failures. I want you to be aware of just how sweet success can be.

My own field of moonlighting happens to be commercial real estate and my single project last year was to develop a small shopping center. I will net approximately $250,000 for the effort. This year I'm developing a larger one. You will learn the *how to* aspects of starting a sideline business later, along with many possibilities that are suitable for moonlighting, but let's first look at some reasons why.

Up to now you have not made any business decisions *for yourself*, because job-related decisions are made within the restraints of company policies or committee deliberation. Or, more likely, your boss simply tells you what and what not to do.

As an entrepreneur you will enjoy the pleasure of being president. There is nothing that can build self-esteem more than to have final authority in work. Not until you're in a true leadership role can you fully exercise your intellectual potential to make progress in accomplishing your aims. You can take it from Goethe: "Whatever you can do, or dream you can, begin it. Boldness has genius, power, and magic in it." And so does presidency.

Playing the role of entrepreneur can provide a marvelous contrast from the frustrations inherent in salaried jobs. It will offset the muddy compromises one must wade through when working for others. It will provide the opportunity for self-realization that eludes us at work. The exercise of final authority will revitalize your mental and physical powers and tap into resevoirs of strength unrealized during the absence of opportunity. Being president is exhilarating and can properly be described as the sweetest morsel in the candy store.

Life will take on new dimensions because the moonlighter encounters a completely new set of responsibilities. It will be stimulating rather than fatiguing. There will be a new sense of personal recognition and, irrespective of the size of your undertaking, you will enter into the big leagues, called *business enterprise*. You will be dealing with accountants, lawyers, and bankers. You'll walk a little differently (taller), take better care of yourself, and have a greater interest in what's going on in the world.

It will be your privilege to make the final decisions on designs, merchandising, pricing, and manufacturing. You can, for possibly the first time in your life, do just what you *like* to do. Most who work in jobs do not have the opportunity to try out their own ideas—you will now. You will unleash layers of energy that you presently are unaware of. It is really quite a turn-on.

For some, a moonlight business will provide the opportunity to get the family involved. Perhaps your husband or wife has expressed a desire to refurbish houses, sell a food product, or open a boutique. A moonlight business happens to be especially suited for family enterprises because of the obvious built-in support and mutual assistance afforded by members of the family: a built-in, already functioning combination of interests. The business will produce not only collective income but also the opportunity to work in harmony for a common cause. Indeed, the economic interdependence of a family business can become the cohesive remedy for the splintered nature of contemporary family life.

Although money is certainly one of the primary reasons for family estrangement, it is interesting that such problems usually do not occur while money is being made. More often they surface after the money is earned and questions come up as to who gets it! Working together in a business will bind families together because the family will share a goal, in contrast to fighting over the proceeds of a will.

Think about the family businesses you happen to be familiar with. Perhaps they include your local nursery or firms with names ending in "and Sons." But it's no longer only "and Sons," because women (more than 50 percent of the college population today) are joining and running family businesses every bit as much as the sons are.

Another advantage of a moonlight business is that you can decide how best to earn money through the exploitation of other people's efforts. You can, for example, set up your accounting system to report profit-and-loss statements for each separate department or component of your business. Your managers can then be compensated on the basis of individual productivity. And if there are problems, you will be the first to know. You could even build your own organization with employees who themselves have a sense of entrepreneurship within their jobs. You don't have to give up any portion of ownership in order to provide incentives to key people. Employees can be fully motivated by profit sharing.

Without diluting ownership in the slightest, you can multiply your personal efforts. Your first operation will serve as a trial run to test your ideas and to learn the do's and don'ts of the business. Once the wrinkles are worked out, you can decide if you want to expand. For example, you could take a retail concept that you have in mind and (after first making it work) turn it into a chain operation.

Cash businesses *leverage* existing capital by taking in money early (upon sale) and paying for the goods later. We always hear about the importance of working capital to a business. Yet it's possible to open a cash business such as a restaurant with very little working capital. The fast-food chains have been called *cash cows* because their cash flow is so welcome to the conglomerates that typically own them; they can actually take money out rather than continue to pour it in.

Although some businesses can operate with little working capital, let me quickly point out that it's unfortunately not the universal case. For example, I am told that a dry-cleaning store requires about six months before it can build enough business to break even. Any reasonably sophisticated moonlighter is going to have determined this before starting. But not all do, and hence the classroom platitude: "Businesses fail because of lack of working capital."

The very establishment of your business is going to allow access to benefits provided by federal and state laws. The Tax Reform Act of 1986 changed and in many ways reduced these inducements. Yet the business owner will always have economic advantages by virtue of being an employer rather than an employee. And however much our legislators modify the depreciation rates, investment tax credits, and capital gains taxes, it is extremely unlikely that the traditional tax privileges enjoyed by American business will ever be nullified.

For example, your business can provide pension-plan benefits. Contributions can be made from before-tax income so that you can build up a tax-deferred retirement nest egg. Although the rules will always be changing, the "special interests" in this case are represented by such a broad base of working people that we can be reasonably sure that some forms of retirement benefits are going to remain for business owners and their employees. The moonlight business will double your pension benefits because of your dual role as employee and employer.

In our stroll through the moonlighter's candy store, there is one department we can call the forbidden fruit section. As Bill Cosby describes it, this all started with Adam and Eve, who found temptation to be irresistible because they were told: "Don't!" You confront the forbidden fruit every time a sale is made. The decision is whether or not to ring it up. The merchant who doesn't ring the sale up avoids sales tax, federal and state income taxes, and even perhaps the payment of percentage rent. When employees are paid in cash, no employee income taxes are withheld or

5

reported, nor are payments made to Social Security, disability insurance, or workers' compensation insurance. This is how many small businesses are running circles around the larger chain operators, who must obey every letter of the law. The infamous two-martini lunch, symbolic of how Uncle Sam pays for high living, is a small beer in comparison with other ways small business owners can cheat.

In other parts of the world, cheating in business is so common that it has created separate underground economies. In Italy, 32 percent of the labor force is part of the *lavoro nero* (black labor), which goes unreported and untaxed. If everything were official, the social charges alone would add 50 percent to every salary. Amitore Fanfane, five times Italy's prime minister, said: "It's simply a rebellion against the excessive waste of the welfare state. In Italy, the government looks with pragmatic benevolence on the underground economy, and if any administration were so unwise to try to clamp down, it would be an economic disaster."

Obviously the United States has not yet become transformed into a kind of socialistic state such as Italy. And the IRS does not look with "pragmatic benevolence" on underground earnings. Always bear in mind the IRS proverb, "Pigs get fat and hogs get slaughtered." It can be far more productive to focus one's energies on making money rather than on playing the risky game of cheating. The answer is to report every single penny of income you earn and at the same time, aggressively, be sure you utilize every single benefit the tax code allows.

Are all the benefits of being in business worth the risks we take? I would say yes. The moonlight entrepreneur that I envision can enjoy the benefits and at the same time carefully limit the downside risks. If you follow the rules laid out in the following chapters carefully, you are not going to lose your job. Retaining your career is part of the overall plan.

I also firmly believe that now is, historically, the right time. First, the economy is becoming more service-oriented; while employment is shrinking in manufacturing industries, it is expanding healthily in service businesses. Service businesses can be small and flexible, thus offering a wide spectrum of opportunities.

For moonlighters interested in manufacturing, it is no longer necessary to build capital-intensive plants and struggle with all the complexities of labor and production. Entrepreneurs are emerging as the intermediaries between the markets for goods and the centers of production, which may be anywhere in the world.

Lewis Anten, who is my patent lawyer, and his partner, Arnie Rubin, started a new toy company they called Funrise. Eighteen months later one of their products was number two on the best-seller lists of toys sold in America. It was all done without factories or overhead. Lewis handles the legal work and Arnie comes up with the ideas, but the designs, tooling, production, and packaging are all subcontracted to vendors in Hong Kong and China (and, by now, heaven knows where else).

I recently bought a new tennis ball machine made by Prince Manufacturing Company. On a small nameplate, I discovered that the machine was assembled in Mexico. The parts may have been made in Taiwan! Prince doesn't need a factory to make those machines; all it needs is the knowledge of the market and the capability to design, subcontract, and put together the parts. You can be in big business without plant or equipment at all; a fax machine, a telephone, and a knowledge of international trade will do.

Specialization has become the key to success for many moonlighters who can undercut the costs and better the performance of larger companies. Complexity in our lives has also created new businesses. My next-door neighbor is in business for himself as a consultant for toxic waste handling. Today every service station that is demolished must have the soil analyzed for toxic contamination—presto—a new industry is born for the alert entrepreneur.

Government agencies are finding that private industry can perform functions for them more cheaply than civil servants can. As a result, widespread privatization of government functions has proved to be an opportunity for new businesses. The city where I live doesn't have a plan-check department anymore because it is done more efficiently by a private engineering firm. Who runs the firm? Former, "retired," city plan checkers and structural engineers.

One thing I have taken pains not to say is that starting a business is easy; it is not. But there is no great fun derived from doing something that is effortless, riskless. As John Wooden has said, "Failure is not fatal but failure to change might be." Thank God that we are free to choose and that the choices for the moonlighter are so abundant.

# CHAPTER TWO

# A Good Job (Nowadays) is Hard to Find

Surely a worthwhile reason to moonlight would be to make enough money to ensure a comfortable retirement. For those who must depend entirely on their jobs, this objective is getting a bit uncertain. *Fortune* magazine faced this problem in its cover-story article of July 1989 entitled "Will You Be Able To Retire?" In the past, retirement income has been a three-legged stool: We have relied on Social Security, private pensions, and savings.

But nowadays, as *Fortune* points out, all three of these legs are getting a bit wobbly. Social Security's maximum benefit is presently only $10,788. Company pension plans are being curtailed as firms realize that present and future earnings can be hobbled by retirement benefit commitments. For example, in 1989 Merrill Lynch terminated a generous pension plan in favor of a less costly one and booked a $220 million after-tax gain as a result. And as for savings, we're no longer able to save anywhere near enough for maintaining our lifestyles in retirement. Moonlight earnings, salted away in your *own* pension plan, can help close this gap.

There is yet another reason to moonlight: it could be your parachute if your job goes down in flames. Many employers are cutting pension benefits because they face more and more difficulties competing with low-cost rivals throughout the world. In a protest held in New York City, an unemployed worker showed up in a barrel with the sign: "My job has gone overseas."

One popular American-made lock sells for $5.95 alongside another made in Taipei selling for $3.95. An American-made adjustable wrench ($15.95) is displayed next to an adjustable wrench from China that sells for $4.89. American workers have good reason to think about moonlighting!

A great number of American industries are solving this problem by becoming hollow corporations; that is, closing their factories and replacing them with subcontractors in other parts of the world. This may spell survival for the company, but it also spells pink slips for the employees. A story in *Business Week* was entitled, "The End of Corporate Loyalty?" It didn't refer to disloyalty on the part of employees but to the fact that corporations in America have gone on a crash diet. They are cutting away layer after layer of management in order to survive. Corporations no longer keep employees on the payroll in lean times as well as fat.

If you work for a large company, your management is perhaps mulling over executive retrenchment plans. Diminishing profits are shored up by peeling off layers of expensive middle managers. "Downsizing" and "restructuring" is the name of the game now. No wonder Chrysler emerged as a strong firm: it cut nearly half of the salaried employees, lowering the break-even point from 2.4 million cars and trucks to 1.2 million units.

Your own firm won't be reluctant to eliminate your job now that it's in such distinguished company as AT&T, Eastman Kodak, and General Electric. In fact, white-collar layoffs are now ethically acceptable on management's part. And no business or profession is exempt from this trend. Even the accounting profession has undergone mergers, bringing turmoil into the ranks of the (formerly) Big Eight firms. In 1989, the Big Eight became the Big Six with the mergers of Ernst & Whinney and Arthur Young into Ernst & Young, and Deloitte Haskins & Sells and Touche Ross into Deloitte & Touche. Both firms have pushed out at least 5 percent of partners. And as audit businesses continue to shrink, CPAs are slashing fees and cutting staffs.

Leveraged buyouts leave no safety in small firms either. Changes in ownership can catch long-time employees by complete surprise. A friend of mine was general manager of the Beverly Hills Hotel and was very good at his job. In a partnership buyout deal, the hotel was sold out and my friend suddenly found himself without a job.

Both small and large firms are also slashing employment because of more stringent mandates called for by safety agencies, air-quality regulations, or more stringent labor laws. The furniture manufacturing business in southern California has all but disappeared because firms cannot afford to install equipment required by the Air Quality Management Districts. Where have the jobs gone? In most cases, to Mexico.

Chain retailers are realizing that franchised or independently run stores can operate profitably at much lower levels of sales. The independent operators can strip away layer after layer of expense. Chains must now either limit their operations to very large stores and at the same time either sell off, sublease, or franchise the small ones.

Our jobs are threatened by more than hard times. In the best of times, we have the all too familiar takeovers, spinoffs, and mergers. Managers are bailing out or getting eased, pushed, or kicked out faster and more often. Companies are paying such high takeover prices that their first step is to reduce costs to justify the merger. The mountains of debt must be serviced by "increased operating efficiencies." As Robert Lamalie of the New York executive search firm of Lamalie Associates observes, "they immediately have to come up with efficiencies to get profits up and one way is to wipe out parts of the organization." Cash flow is king, and it is an unhappy and sobering fact that even the most prestigious of companies can no longer be relied upon to guarantee permanent work.

And the irony is that those who have it best now could be the ones most likely to suffer. I know a young man who works in a major motion-picture studio. He earns about $80,000 a year splicing sound tracks onto film. Now, I think his job is too good to be true. Already, American independent producers are beginning to go abroad or to subcontract to nonunion shops.

Mike Douglas explained why he filmed abroad: "It was cheaper." He didn't have to pay enormous salaries or 40 percent fringe benefits. The moral is that if you have it especially good in your job, you're probably a prime moonlighting candidate because someday your employer is going to figure out how to do your job more cheaply.

Stop and ask yourself this: Does your own job provide a secure base from which to undertake a moonlight activity? A good job means being in the right business, the right company, and the right slot within the company. Being in the right business means that you are in an industry that is healthy and not threatened by technical or strategic extinction. And you will have to be bluntly objective in making this evaluation. As of 1991 the savings and loan industry might not be considered a "right" business, because of its need for a massive government bailout program. The doughnut business today is not a "right" business because of changing dietary habits and the entry into the breakfast market by the big fast-food chains and convenience stores.

You can judge for yourself if you're working for the right company. This can be measured by the relative strengths of your own employer with other firms in your business. For example, if you were in the steel business, you would probably feel good about working for Nucor Steel. Nucor can match or beat the price of its competition, including the Japanese, by combining new technology with productivity incentives for its workers. It has also made Nucor employees the best paid and most secure anywhere.

To decide if you are in the right slot within your company, you can judge how your company creates a productive atmosphere for you. There is a yardstick for deciding this question that is used by motivational experts. They maintain that people do a better job when the employer fulfills the following five needs:

- ▸ Economic security
- ▸ Emotional security
- ▸ Recognition
- ▸ Self-expression
- ▸ Self-respect

Your present job will measure up or it will not. If your job is worth holding onto (even if you happen to be frustrated in your career), always remember the moonlighter's revenge: it's *you* who will be the boss after the whistle blows. But if you find yourself in the wrong job, you should relocate into a good one before you begin to march the moonlight trail. And if your firm is in financial difficulty, plan your exit *before* the company gets into still deeper trouble.

You may ask why anyone would stick with a failing company. It's done all the time. One reason is morbid fascination about the outcome of events we are involved in, and another is the camaraderie of everyone defending the fort against overpowering forces. The curiosity of a hanging (even our own), a sense of loyalty, and the inertia of not wanting to make the tough decision to bail out work together to keep people on a sinking ship. To reposition yourself into a better situation takes courage and initiative.

And if these aren't enough reasons to moonlight, consider how secure your job will be in a recession-dominated economy. The 1990s are shaping up to become the protracted bursting of the speculative bubble of the 1980s. In the global economy of the 1990s, resources, capital, and technology will strengthen contacts around the world (to the benefit of nimble entrepreneurs). What will not develop mobility so quickly is the work force.

Many U.S. job holders are being asked to accept the same pay their counterparts receive in Korea, because General Motors can (and does) build cars in Korea. This explains why the U.S. Department of Labor reported that among the "non-supervisory work force" (2/3 of the total), between 1973 and 1990 wages fell eighteen percent on a weekly basis when adjusted to the cost-of-living index.

Economic growth is the only answer to this slump, yet in 1991 productivity in the United States was dropping 1 percent per year—and population only growing at the rate of 1/2 percent per year. For recovery, something has to boom. Yet it will not be defense, construction, retail, banking, or electronics. And taxes aren't going down; they're going up. This means that we're in for stagnant income gains in the 1990s, and there won't be rapid growth in jobs even if the recession disappears.

No matter how you earn a living, there are enemies threatening your job. Yet the alternative of going into a business would probably bring on an acute case of the heebie jeebies in even the best of us. From the seemingly secure vantage point of holding a job, going into a full-time business has some genuinely frightening elements, including fear of failure, the loss of job security, and the risk of losing the family jewels.

Who needs it? Those who are secure in their jobs don't, but if your job disappears, you'll have an entirely different perspective. It's like the toad who got himself lodged in a deep rut while hopping across a coun-

11

try road. Hop and scramble as he would, he only became exhausted. Friends offered advice but to no avail, and they went sadly away. The next morning, to their astonishment, they met the toad hopping along, more chipper than ever. "But you couldn't get out!" they exclaimed. "I know I couldn't," he replied, "but a truck came along and I had to!"

There is a truck coming down our road and your job may end up in a ditch, and I want to get your adrenaline pumped up so that you can jump out of it. When you think about it, many success stories about entrepreneurs start out by saying they *had to* because there were no jobs available. Consider the Chinese who fled their homeland in 1949. Some escaped to Hong Kong, where they didn't have the option of finding a job or going into business. There were no jobs, so they became entrepreneurs. They had no choice other than to jump out of their rut and into businesses.

A proverb reminds us that "a prudent man foresees the difficulties ahead and prepares for them; the simpleton goes blindly on and suffers the consequences." For us, survival options do not fit into simple alternatives. And if we're not secure in having a good job, where will we find it? The normal working person develops a paralyzing ambivalence: apprehensive on the one hand of job security yet intimidated on the other hand by the hazards of going into business. Full-bore entrepreneurship is a way out. But it's not an easy way, because it's simply too traumatic and frightening a transition for the great majority of us.

The free enterprise system gives us a choice: we can either work for someone else or work for ourselves. Or, and this is my main point, we can *do both*. The answer is to keep your job and at the same time start a moonlight business of your own.

# CHAPTER THREE

# Your Full-Time Job Won't Suffer

You may fear that moonlighting in a business will result in poor marks in your other job. As much as you (or your employer) may believe that moonlighters are frequently absent and perform poorly, the fact is that, according to recent university research, this is simply not true. The study concerned employees who held second jobs rather than those who operated moonlight businesses; for our purposes, it is not unreasonable to extrapolate the results to the latter category as well.

Dr. Muhammad Jamal, a management professor at Concordia University in Montreal, conducted the research among 939 people, and his conclusion was that "there was virtually no difference between moonlighters and non-moonlighters in job performance, rate of turnover, and absenteeism." Dr. Jamal also found that on the social level, moonlighters rated higher for membership in voluntary organizations and participating in volunteer work. On the personal level, there is no difference between moonlighters and non-moonlighters in job stress and marital happiness; but in job satisfaction, moonlighters scored higher. He also said that his findings would pertain to the United States as well as Canada.

In addition, Dr. Jamal stated that past studies found moonlighters to be "more emotionally stable, less anxious, more realistic, and more active" than non-moonlighters. "They're very well-organized, not time wasters," he reported. "The average moonlighter works only fourteen hours extra a week, yet the average American watches TV for twenty-five hours a week. Instead of sitting in front of the tube, the person who moonlights is spending his extra hours working—which will give him more experience and money, enrich his social circle, and make him more active."

Although it is evident that there are many opportunities for employees to moonlight in other jobs, there is also plenty of room left for moonlighters who opt for running a business on the side. In fact, approximately 1.3 million new businesses are started every year in the United States.

The difference between choosing to take a second job and choosing to run a moonlight business can be measured in terms of entrepreneurial desire. This is the engine that will pull you into running a business rather than working a second job. You shouldn't need vocational guidance to determine whether your mind is set on entrepreneurship; if you're hot, you're hot—and if you're not, you're not.

I have already mentioned the current wave of immigrants, many of whom are paragons of entrepreneurship. But keep in mind that in most cases they're in business because, historically, survival has left them no alternative; it's the only proven way of making a decent living. Yet Americans of all ages and backgrounds are candidates for operating a business—including the increasing numbers of those older than sixty who continue working and who surely have the requisite money and experience.

As a director of a non-profit foundation that sponsors entrepreneurial seminars, I frequently receive letters saying things such as "I would like information regarding your program. I'm a sixty-three-year-old man thinking of retirement but would like to stay active." So why *not* a small business on the side for someone like this who works at a job but has an unrequited entrepreneurial strain? And, as Dr. Jamal reports, keeping active beats watching TV.

Operating a business that is completely unrelated to your job skills or commitments will further minimize the risks of job disruption. What began in the kitchen or garage as a hobby can become your starting point—for example, cheesecake, designer sweat shirts, or artistic novelties. Do whatever you can do on the side that answers the magic question: Is there a need (even a whimsical one), and can I fill it?

A job that leaves you with ample and well-defined free time is especially appropriate for moonlighting. For example, you will be less subject to criticism if you only work four days per week (perhaps ten hours per day), because you can schedule your business activities around the remaining free time. If you work at night you're free to moonlight during normal business hours in the daytime. Moonlighters who enjoy the inherent stability of government positions, public service, and teaching jobs have an even smaller chance of suffering from the raised eyebrows of the boss.

But if your boss does look askance at your moonlighting activities, don't forfeit a good job by resigning impetuously. Cultivate in yourself the capacity to accept and deflect the raised eyebrows of management, and to shrug off the disappointments. Sometimes the temptation to quit—the easy solution—can become overpowering, and it only takes two words to escape: "I quit!" Yet if your job is secure and not suffering as a result of your moonlighting, it is better to take a break and think it over. To quit is like pulling the pin of a hand grenade; once you've done it, your only choice is to duck.

Those who quit their jobs because of the boss's misguided opinion of moonlighting will not have the chance to clear up any of these misconceptions. You might consider the alternative of going to your employer, explaining Dr. Jamal's findings, and asserting that your outside activities are adding energy and commitment to your life—including, of course, your job. If you are sincere, this kind of upfront encounter will, more often than not, be met with an effort to work things out.

If you have *serious* problems with your employer, you might ask to be transferred into a completely new position. Your reasons should be truthful, yet stated so as to make clear that you wish to stay rather than leave and that you wish to pursue your moonlight activity as well. Put yourself in the place of your employer; if the tables were turned, would *you* want to support an ambitious employee who wished to stay with you and who sincerely confronted you with such a request?

Now, there are some instances where Dr. Jamal's findings, as encouraging as they are for most of us, simply do not work for others, and in fairness this must be pointed out. Moonlighting is not going to be appropriate for employees whose jobs entail awesome responsibilities or provide equally awesome benefits. Neither will moonlighting be appropriate for those who may not have top-brass jobs but whose incentive compensation packages include a commission or profit-sharing arrangement that requires full commitment both during and outside normal business hours.

For example, my former partner, Frank Watase, was once hired by a large conglomerate to take over as vice president of several retail merchandising divisions. His compensation included stock options as well as 10 percent of the before-tax earnings of his divisions.

Now, while Frank was enormously zealous in pursuing his job and quite successful in accomplishing a turnaround, at the same time he began a moonlight real estate venture with his brother to develop a high-rise office building. Problems developed because this real estate venture was one of high public visibility and began showing up in the newspapers. Under these circumstances, the employer simply couldn't tolerate Frank's dual role. Frank finally gave up his job rather than give up the moonlighting. So, as you can see, there are exceptions.

Some top managers are making such gigantic salaries and bonuses in their corporate jobs that it would be silly to start *anything* on the side. When corporate managers have big buck incentives, there is normally enough authority and recognition attached to the job that they don't need the satisfaction of running their own businesses, because they are already running someone else's. And they are reaping the rewards without incurring the risks.

Recently I've had the pleasure of visiting the senior offices at the top of the ARCO building and observing how top managers work in this kind of environment. (It is very stimulating to see, believe me.) They are masters of "intrapreneurship," the buzzword coined by Gifford Pinchot to refer to the practice of entrepreneurship within a corporate structure.

**15**

I *know* these people are paid enormously well, and my guess is that they don't need the challenge of starting their own deals at all.

However, this is not the case for the vast majority of the rest of us down on the lower floors. We are going to obtain our true satisfaction—and make our money—outside our nine-to-five jobs. Our hats should be off to Dr. Muhammad Jamal, whose research can show us (as well as our bosses) that full-time jobs *don't* suffer when employees moonlight.

# PART TWO ▼ HOW

Here are practical pointers on how to juggle your
job and your business without getting tripped up.

# CHAPTER FOUR

# The Moonlight Juggling Act

$B$efore we begin looking at specific moonlighting ideas, let's first understand that you're about to get into a juggling act. You will have the intoxicating and ongoing thrill of spinning plates in the air, each propelled onward by the meticulously timed flicking of a stick. You will be spinning two plates: your job and your moonlight business. You will learn some techniques here that will keep both activities moving with the necessary momentum.

The very essence of the moonlight juggling act is to keep up with your job while you play the entrepreneur on the side. Going "all the way" doesn't mean tendering your resignation, yet most entrepreneurs don't look at it this way. The traditional attitude is one of full commitment.

I recently met a fellow who had just returned from a tour of duty in Europe as a manager for the Mobil Corporation. His career at Mobil had gained him economic rewards, including a big salary, a pension plan, and a generous assortment of other perks. He had been with Mobil for ten years, and upon his return to the United States was planning to resign in order to go into business. He was busily attending business opportunity shows, talking with franchisors, and looking up businesses for sale in the classified section of the newspaper.

With typical entrepreneurial zeal, he had given no thought to the strategy of the moonlight juggler. He was planning to resign from Mobil because he assumed that entrepreneurs are expected to burn their bridges behind them. Believe me, his approach was not at all uncommon and is, in fact, the standard approach of most who start up businesses.

The moonlight juggler's strategy discards this approach. Forget it. You're going to be a juggler instead: a plate spinner. And the delicious and seemingly illicit paradox of being a juggler is that whereas juggling implies an inherently unstable act, juggling a business on the side is a *far* safer approach than quitting your job and going full bore into business. It is far better to scratch the entrepreneurial itch outside the job . . . without jeopardizing everything that goes with it.

You might say, "Why would anyone do anything so foolish as to quit a good job anyway?" Let me assure you that it's done all the time. People are propelled into starting businesses by what I call "entrepreneurial guts."

Although this instinct motivates us, it doesn't always motivate us to be prudent. Indeed, you have probably seen, as I have, too many cases of entrepreneurs who possess more guts than brains.

The moonlight juggler, on the other hand, combines the guts trait to get started in a business with the simple safety measure of staying in the nine-to-five job as well. This changes everything. It is no longer a matter of all or nothing. The juggler's chance of success is greater because not only is the safety net still there but also the new business is undertaken in a much more calculated mode.

Assuming for the moment that you're in a reasonably stable job and that you use the cautious approach spelled out in this book, then at no time will you be exposed to complete failure. What the future holds will depend on the outcome of your job, or your business, or both.

For example, the Mobil executive could start a sideline business without even thinking of quitting his job. After a while, were Mobil to offer him a promotion or challenge too good to turn down, his moonlight venture could be phased out. Perhaps his new business would have blossomed, encouraging him to abandon his job in order to expand as a full-time entrepreneur. As a moonlight juggler, he would begin from a position of safety, leaving future options open so that he can pursue whatever activities are producing optimum results.

This juggling act must start with a three-step plan. The first step is to write out clearly what your new business plan will be. Analyze the problems of your industry. Determine what your own strengths and weaknesses are. The idea is to leverage your strengths and to correct your weaknesses. Your business plan should also include an analysis of the unsatisfied needs of your potential customers.

Never make the assumption that your product is going to be a world beater. There may be a vast gulf between your concept of a winning idea and what the public will buy. Honestly, you really don't know. The only way to find out is to go out yourself, order book in hand, and get some feedback. Now your business plan is based on reality and not concept. Never, *never* start what you have not first tested eyeball-to-eyeball with your potential customers.

The last reason to set up the manufacture of a product is merely that you know how to make it or have the necessary equipment. Instead, your attention should be concentrated on fulfilling the needs of your customers. By writing out a comprehensive plan, you can achieve one vital requirement: *focus*. You must be focused on and dedicated to fulfilling the specific objectives of your business plan.

Second, you must recruit the key people you will need. Remember that while a circus juggler can keep any number of plates in the air all at once, you can't. You need key people to juggle your business plate while you are at work juggling the plate that is your anchor to security.

**20**

I suggest that your key people should be compensated by commission or by bottom-line profit and loss participation whenever possible. The greatest motivator (for the right kind of manager) is compensation for productivity. A long-term accounting employee of mine was competent and dutiful in every assigned job... that is, until I gave her a $1,000 reward for every sale escrow that she handled. After years of quiet but indifferent efficiency, she turned into a whirlwind of driving zeal to close each escrow.

Part of the job of recruiting key people is designing a suitable incentive plan. As long as the incentive is a function of your net earnings, you can't get tripped up in a situation where the key employee makes a lot of money while you are going broke. For example, I had no problem offering an important department head 10 percent of the business's profit as a bonus, because for every dollar he made, the company made nine.

If you plan to start a family business (covered later in this book), you'll already have some participating jugglers who can help keep those plates spinning. Perhaps a partnership will be the way to go, as long as you work toward common goals and combine complementary talents. Regardless of the proposed size and structure of your business, key people are going to be needed. A moonlight business is not a solo act.

Keep in mind that while you will need to recruit people to whom you can delegate responsibility, you can only delegate what you already know how to do by yourself. If you're starting a business with which you haven't had hands-on experience, don't even think of hiring a person to fulfill a key role. The answer is to learn about the business first by moonlighting in a job to learn the ropes—then delegate.

You should have a clear idea of what credentials your key management people have so you can be objective when interviewing them and not be swayed by a forceful personality or outstanding ability in one aspect of the job. You should look for managers who are

- Well-educated
- Experienced in your specific business field
- Good with people, possessing strong communication skills
- Motivated by compensation for productivity rather than by fixed salary and fringe benefits
- The right age and attitude for your specific business field

Step number three in your juggling act is to be tough and frugal in every one of your decisions. You don't need new equipment if used equipment will do the job. Learn to say "no" or "I'll think about it" whenever you have a financial decision to make. You're going into business to please yourself, not to gain admiration or appreciation from vendors. Many who start out feel that they must go first class—not so. Pretend that you have short arms and low pockets in every decision you make.

Winston Churchill is a good example of a successful moonlight juggler. Before he became prime minister of Great Britain in 1939, he paid for his opulent lifestyle by moonlighting at his writing table. He was a member of Parliament during the daytime and a writer at night. His moonlight plate spinning went on from 11:00 P.M. to 3:00 A.M. every night.

For Churchill, deciding on a moonlight business plan was easy because he could write exceptionally well about either history or current events and he had things to say for which publishers and newspaper editors were willing to pay dearly. He could not have succeeded, however, had he not accomplished step two: he recruited a number of people to help him in his moonlight work. He had three (low-paid) secretaries and a platoon of students who were eager to help with the necessary research.

Although he was not very successful at step three—the exercise of frugality and prudence in business decisions—he was so successful in the first two steps that his income from moonlight writing subsidized his lavish spending habits and carried him through some very difficult years until he finally emerged as the great "Last Lion" to guide England successfully through the Second World War.

It is true that juggling requires alertness and energy, but keep in mind that it can also be a lot of fun. Look at it as a game; just keep those two plates spinning in the air. Remember that you will need some help to keep that entrepreneurial plate spinning up there.

# How to Avoid Conflict of Interest

*For neither you nor anyone else can serve two masters. You will hate one and show loyalty to the other, or else the other way around—you will be enthusiastic about one and despise the other.*

Luke 16:13

All of humanity has struggled with conflict of interest. This will be your foremost problem as a moonlighter and if it is taken lightly or ignored, both your job and your business will be jeopardized. A moonlighter must therefore identify potential conflicts between the responsibilities of work and those running a sideline business.

Our society is full of work-related conflicts; these have become so widespread that laws have been devised to protect public welfare. By law, a doctor may not own a pharmacy and therefore is relieved of any temptation to over-prescribe drugs. Real estate brokers who deal on their own accounts must disclose this to prospective buyers or sellers. The Securities and Exchange Commission prohibits insider trading in securities, yet even the threat of imprisonment has not prevented abuse.

Employers cannot depend on legislation to prevent conflict-of-interest problems, but rather must rely on their own written (or unwritten) policy. For example, it is generally accepted practice that relatives not be allowed to work for one another, because family interest could well be put ahead of the company's.

Yet many grey areas surround the issue and conflicts can arise whether or not regulations, either legal or corporate, are in force. For instance, when the Chamber of Commerce in Palm Springs sponsors an automobile road race, is it proper for them to employ off-duty city police officers? Would this suggest to police officers that they should feel free to moonlight in their own security businesses, if they so desire?

In some jobs, moonlighting is not only accepted; it is standard practice. Firefighters and airline pilots, who work long shifts followed by two or three days off, commonly engage in outside businesses. Everyone knows and approves of this. It is perfectly acceptable for college professors to undertake consulting work and to publish books. Business executives are paid director's fees for spending time on other companies' boards of directors. It is normal practice for public officials to accept honoraria for speaking engagements.

It is not only the pursuit of extra money that can cause conflict of interest in your work. There are other motives as well. For example, purely unselfish causes can interfere with your normal working hours. I know a fellow who was employed full-time and yet contrived to run a construction project for his church at the same time. Over the months during which the church was being built, his responsibilities as a volunteer forced him to deal with other matters during working hours.

Conflict-of-interest issues can pop up in any situation. Lee Iacocca, the president of Chrysler, was in charge of fund-raising for the restoration of the Statue of Liberty. He was also a member of the statue's management commission. Iacocca not only devoted a great deal of time but also contributed millions of dollars of his own money to this worthwhile activity. While the merit of this cause is beyond criticism, could his involvement possibly have conflicted with his responsibilities to Chrysler? Perhaps not, yet the Secretary of the Interior removed Iacocca from the management commission because of "potential conflict of interest" between raising money for the statue and having a responsibility in its management.

Many people are engaged in part-time jobs in order to make ends meet. Working at a second job has never been considered a clandestine activity, but keep in mind that the boss might not regard a moonlight entrepreneur with the same degree of admiration as the person who just holds down a second job. Your employer's worst possible fear would be that you might start a moonlight operation in competition with the business supplying your paycheck. In that case, your employer would be justified in putting his foot down; how can you work for someone and compete with them at the same time?

It must be admitted that whenever we engage in a moonlight activity resulting in a conflict with our job, we cheat our employers. An employee can rationalize this kind of cheating in many ways. In some cases, the absence of company rules to the contrary will be taken as tacit approval. Very few employers have taken a stand on what outside activities will be considered as a conflict with the employee's job responsibilities.

Most companies rely on unwritten policies so as not to create discontent among employees. Labor laws are liberally interpreted by courts to protect workers. As a result, employers are hesitant to institute policies that could result in lawsuits by employees claiming unfair treatment or discrimination.

Many jobs, such as those involving outside sales, cannot be closely supervised, and this also invites conflict of interest. The difficulty lies in human nature; we are all too likely to place our own interest above that of our employer. An unhappy employee can rationalize a conflict because of some grudge held against the employer stemming from broken promises, unrealized expectations, or the feeling that the company is not providing sufficient pay and benefits. In fact, the employer can be (and is) blamed for any and every disappointment in the workplace.

The prospective moonlighters should not be guided simply by what opportunity will allow, nor can a course of action be dictated by the work environment or the absence of employer policy. The solution is to develop an operating format that strictly separates work life from entrepreneurial life. You must first recognize the following three factors when evaluating your situation for conflicts:

- It will be difficult to be objective.
- You will be restricted as to what kind of moonlight business to engage in.
- A moonlight business in conflict with your job will blow up your job.

The overall strategy is to create two separate compartments for your working life: the job and the moonlight venture. For each compartment, maintain a separate integrity with respect to time, thought, place, and business. This takes a great deal of discipline to implement.

Some businesses will conflict with your job and others will not. This will limit your field of endeavor and may even prevent you from going into a business of your choice. A prospective business must be judged not only in terms of the prospects for success, but also in terms of conflict with your regular work. Businesses with a high likelihood of creating conflict of interest include those with the following general characteristics:

- Labor-intensive
- Conducted during hours you normally work
- 24-hour responsibility
- Requiring travel
- Requiring long hours

Sometimes these problems can be overcome by a married couple or by partners; your spouse or partner takes on the business responsibility while you're at work. If you work during normal business hours in a job, any moonlight business requiring your personal attention at that time is going to be a problem—after all, it's called *moonlighting* presumably because it takes place after hours. Unless you are set up with qualified managers, this rules out opening any business that must be conducted during your own working hours.

On the brighter side, there are other business opportunities that can be operated successfully without running against your job. The characteristics of an appropriate moonlight business (when judged for conflict of interest) include:

► Merchandising by mail, telephone, or computer
► Time spent can be dictated by yourself rather than by your customers or business hours
► Family members can help and fill in
► Hollow corporations (covered in Chapter 12)

Here are some moonlight operations that are examples of businesses probably not in conflict with a working career:

| Business | Why Appropriate |
|---|---|
| A single product | Specialization reduces conflicting situations |
| Real estate | An activity you can do on your own time, in your own place |
| Specialized food | Production can start in your kitchen: peanut brittle, cookies, pasta, etc. |
| Direct marketing | Your time, your place |
| A proprietary product | Can be handled in your garage or contracted out to others |
| A family-run business | Built-in backup and an already in-place organization |

Selling houses may yield more than selling peanut brittle, unless your peanut brittle is irresistibly good and so well marketed that your name becomes the generic word for the product. Mrs. Field's cookies were started in her kitchen, as were Knott's Berry Farms jams; there are hundreds of other examples. You don't necessarily need to aim low; there are opportunities for everyone.

Here are some helpful examples of both conflicting and non-conflicting situations.

The maintenance man in a 350-unit condominium complex is employed (on salary) to make common-area repairs. With the full approval of the board of directors, he is also available to condominium owners to do repair jobs. He charges the owners on an hourly basis for this work. The board of directors do not understand (yet) the conflict between his job and his moonlighting for owners. As time goes on, chances are that things will get worse. More and more of his time will be spent working for the owners on an hourly basis, and as he is already receiving a fixed salary from the association, they will get less and less from him.

As you can see, not all employees are free to moonlight, whether they have the approval of the boss or not. I can take some examples of this from my former firm, Yum Yum Donut Shops. Some Yum Yum employees can become moonlighters and others cannot. There is an explicit understanding with store managers that they are to avoid engaging in outside business activities, because there's no way to run a store and find sufficient time to run another business. The demands on their time are great and the hours are irregular. On the other hand, bakers and counter persons are free to become moonlight entrepreneurs, and there is no way the company could legitimately object to their doing so.

One Yum Yum employee, Greg Barnwell, worked in the central manufacturing center and had an interesting second career in moonlighting. In the summer of 1984, he purchased a Chrysler limousine that he rented out to visitors who had come to Los Angeles to see the Olympic Games. That's a pretty good display of entrepreneurial spirit, right? His moonlight business was not a permanent thing, and he disclosed it to everyone. He was proud of what he was doing.

Greg then went into another moonlight business: the buying and management of apartment buildings. He started with a duplex and then traded up to a seven-unit. This did not conflict with his job at Yum Yum, either. Finally, his entrepreneurial drive took charge completely, and he left the firm to begin manufacturing the same product line he had supervised earlier in his job. That's an example of moonlight entrepreneuring becoming the stepping stone to a full-bore business operation. Without ever having conflict-of-interest problems trip him up along the way, he was able to start part time and, as his confidence and skills grew, mature into a full-time business operator. I'm very proud of him!

Another employee, a bookkeeper, is a moonlight writer interested in writing television scripts and working industriously at this activity. Here is a clear case of an inherently non-conflicting activity. He has the good sense to compartmentalize his writing activities completely outside of his job. You will not, I trust, see him in the copy room running off manuscripts.

One form of moonlighting popular today is to become engaged in direct sales, such as with Amway products. I find this kind of activity perfectly acceptable, unless you make the common error of selling to other employees on company time. Very simply, it all comes down to a single rule: the successful moonlighter leads a compartmentalized life.

Nothing in the moonlight business can be allowed to impose on the time or loyalty which is due your employer. Every responsibility of the primary job must be fulfilled, hopefully in more than full measure. A protective shield must be erected around the job to protect the trust to which your employer is entitled. It is easy to deliberately (or quite

**27**

innocently) pierce this shield. Using your employer's telephone for your moonlight business is a signal of impending disaster.

If your employer has a policy against moonlighting, the decision becomes whether to resign and work for someone else who has no such objection, or to forgo the sideline business altogether. If an employer does not have rules regarding conflict of interest, I don't think it's necessary to ask permission before starting a moonlight business. It becomes a matter of judgment on your part to decide if such a disclosure is appropriate or not.

The following guidelines can help you avoid mistakes that can destroy everything you're setting out to accomplish. Here are the ground rules:

- Be available to spend as much time on the job as is required.
- Ensure that no time will be spent on the job for the moonlight business.
- Ensure that no job facilities will be used for the moonlight business.
- Do not compete with your employer.
- Do not start a business unless you have enough time away from the job to do it right.
- The moonlight business must lend itself to being compartmentalized well away from the job.

A conflicting moonlight business will ultimately destabilize your life. The only alternatives to disaster are to solve the conflict or abandon the idea of a moonlight business altogether. If you are emotionally unable to make the necessary division between job and business, you will be torn apart by stress and run a high risk of failing in everything.

Obviously, your moonlight business should complement your life and not destroy it. If you follow my advice, you won't be serving two masters at all; instead, you'll experience what it means to have the best of two worlds: the security of a career plus the excitement of being your own boss.

# CHAPTER SIX

# To Quit or Not to Quit

One inescapable decision you'll have to make when going into business is whether to go about it full time or part time. Before you arrive at the point to make this decision, you will need to keep in mind some prerequisites. This chapter will review these prerequisites and will also state the case for not quitting your job at all. If you are now working and want to start a business, you only have two choices: either to resign from your job or to become a moonlight entrepreneur.

As it happens, I have done it both ways and because you will be confronted with the same problems I had, my personal experience may help you. So bear with me for a bit of nostalgia that could prove to be pertinent to your own situation. If it is, I can spare you a great deal of wear and tear. This is the kind of situation where you won't have much chance to gain insights from those who have gone through this experience first hand.

Before getting into this case study, let's consider the four prerequisites required in order to even make such a decision. First of all, you will need to have an expanding, passionate, and unrelenting desire to be your own boss. This entrepreneurial eagerness comes in all degrees. Obviously, it will take a great deal more ardor to quit altogether than will be required to motivate you into a moonlight business. There are many who can qualify for moonlighting but who will never be sufficiently motivated to leave their jobs altogether.

Second, you'll need an opportunity. This means having something in mind to do that will qualify as a business. It must be an activity you *want* to do. Also, you will need to be qualified to manage this business.

Third, your idea must be for a product or service that will fill the unsatisfied needs of enough customers to make it a success.

Finally, you'll need a willingness to take on some risks. In order to play, you must step up to the table and put down some money. You'll learn later how to limit your stakes but nevertheless, some of the family fortune will be at risk.

Once all four of these elements are present, you're in a position to make your decision: either go into business full time or on a moonlight basis. Here's how the decision unfolded in my own case. My job was a good one; I was an industrial products sales engineer for Manville Corporation. The job involved contact with mostly small businesses, including wholesalers, contractors, and manufacturers.

Now, over the period of three years during which I held this position, I became more and more appreciative of the roles played by the owners of these businesses. This firsthand exposure to entrepreneurs awakened a desire in me to be in business, somehow, for myself. You might say that the idea of being in business had begun to rub off on me. Once I contracted this desire (or more likely, once the latent desire finally surfaced), it never left me or diminished in force during a lifetime of business pursuits.

Yet to my surprise, my entrepreneurial urge was not shared at all by my fellow workers. While I was busily preoccupied with various plans for starting some kind of a business, my colleagues were more concerned about their jobs, the stock market, or golf. My friends in the sales department in Manville were perfectly content working in their jobs. None, all of whom dealt with the same kind of customers—business owners—that I did, ever succumbed to the entrepreneur's itch.

It's no wonder, because employers can create a working and social environment that quite easily becomes a perfectly acceptable way of life for the great majority of us. Employees can become institutionalized, just like companies. This leads us to that first prerequisite you will need before making the decision to stay or leave: You must be possessed of that pleasantly illicit yet irrepressible itch to be free of the institutionalized way of life.

The next prerequisite that opened up for me was opportunity. At the same time that itch to be free was intensifying, I had become interested in trying my hand at construction. Residential home sales were booming and houses were being sold quickly by even part-time builders. (It was a favorite moonlight activity for firefighters, whose work schedules left them completely free for days.) I was seriously looking for *something* to do on my own, and presto! a new tract of prime residential lots went up for sale in my neighborhood. My opportunity was at hand.

At the time I didn't have an awful lot of money. But I had regularly saved about 15 percent of my income, which gave me *something*. And I was prepared to use all of it for a business; later, when I actually did get started, I borrowed a good deal more from my father-in-law. I was simply not afraid of losing money, because the possibility of losing it didn't even occur to me. This is part of the (not always prudent) makeup of an entrepreneur. But, on the other hand, the *fear* of losing money is probably the biggest stumbling block in deterring otherwise-qualified would-be entrepreneurs.

These factors, falling together as they did, became my opening to face the big decision: Do I quit or do I moonlight? For me, all the prerequisites were present: instinct, opportunity, an unsatisfied consumer need, and a willingness to take risks. These elements, thoroughly blended together, will produce an entrepreneur. The desire for money (I wouldn't call it greed) fueled my courage to get started, and later sustained me through the seemingly endless hours of work. The only remaining question was: How to go about it?

Now, at this stage of my career in Manville, I didn't even think about quitting my job; it was too good to give up. Since my work was (for the most part) outside the office, my daily work schedule was pretty much up to me, but I still had a career in mind with the company. I became a moonlight entrepreneur because I was not about to leave my job, yet at the same time I wanted to build houses. I simply went about doing what I had to do.

I figured that the safest approach would be to start with building two houses similar in layout to those currently selling fastest. Between my savings account and my father-in-law's loan, I made the leap and purchased two lots. Then I went to the architect who was designing for the most successful professional builders. Acting as an owner-builder, I then proceeded to build the houses by subcontracting to the various trades. It was an exciting experience that did wonders for my self esteem. Both houses promptly sold, and within twelve months I had made more than my annual earnings as a sales engineer.

Yet a moonlighter's burgeoning career can be upset by changing circumstances in the regular job—in my case, by a quite unforeseen event. I was approached by the national division manager (who had no idea what I was doing on the side) and offered a management job in the New York headquarters. This kind of opportunity did not come often to regional sales representatives. It was like being offered access to the ladder leading to corporate heaven.

My decision was to abandon my first moonlight venture of house building for the opportunity of working in New York. Thus, new job opportunities can complicate the plans of the moonlighter. Promotions will come up all the time in your career, and at the most unexpected of times. In some cases the geographical mobility required by certain careers can make moonlighting quite impractical. IBM has been said to stand for "I've Been Moved": not too appropriate a job format for moonlighting.

My first moonlight career was thus ended by a promotion, yet it had been an unqualified success. The sideline activity did not, luckily, get me into hot water with Manville. Looking back, I can see that had I not been promoted, my house building career would surely have gotten me in trouble with my employer. The fact was that I had really violated conflict-of-interest ethics (but not company regulations) by spending time away from my sales territory to supervise the construction of my houses.

In the clearer perspective of hindsight, I now know it to have been an unstable situation. The hours spent on the moonlight business were, to a large measure, the same as those I would normally spend in my sales territory. In spite of this, the moonlighting activity in some ways actually improved my stature in the company. My co-workers were impressed by my entrepreneurial guts, and my local boss didn't seem to be troubled (or aware) of the conflict with my job.

On the other hand, a good deal of physical stress can be created by holding down a job and a business at the same time, especially when conflict of interest is present. This was what happened in my case. I quickly learned the importance of sticking rigidly to the conflict-of-interest rules. Assuming that you will be clear of this problem, you will then face the following three choices once your business is underway.

Choice 1.   Press on with your job and your business.

Choice 2.   Drop the moonlight activity whenever the nine-to-five one offers greater promise in a way that would make it difficult to continue moonlighting.

Choice 3.   If the moonlight career blossoms, then resign the job and become a full-time entrepreneur.

Any one of these options can be selected without the risk of finding yourself without any means of earning a living. If one option doesn't make sense or is made impractical because of changing circumstances, then another is still available.

Job opportunities or promotions may occur that are simply too good to refuse. As it happened in my case, the opportunity to work in Manville's headquarters in New York was an experience not to be turned down. Had I turned down the promotion, my career would have been completely blocked. To use the exquisitely convincing phrase of management re-cruiting, it was an "investment in my future."

What I ultimately learned from the promotion was that if you're entrepreneurially inclined, there is a special risk to being promoted: you may find an even higher echelon of frustration. Unless, that is, you're at the very top of the pecking order where you become the peckor rather than the peckee, which was surely not the case with me.

But it is also fair to say that entrepreneurs often find it difficult to be happy in a middle-management job, let alone to deal with the politics of a company's headquarters. Some companies may be good at harnessing this kind of energy, but most aren't. More likely, you may find yourself (as I did) in a staid climate where your creative spirit is not nurtured by your supervisors. Of course, I could have satisfied my entrepreneurial yearnings by starting up a moonlight business in New York. However, by this time I was at the mid-management point of my career (and in New York, rather than home in California) and this option—amazingly and perhaps stupidly—simply didn't even occur to me.

I felt that since I had attained a position (however lowly) at the management level, I was left only with the alternatives of sticking with the company or resigning to go into business full time. Keep in mind that this was in spite of my earlier, successful episode of moonlighting in house building while I was a sales representative.

This is not to say that those with an entrepreneurial streak inevitably do poorly at the management level. If my decision were to stay with Manville in management, my entrepreneurial attitude would not necessarily have been a liability at all. In corporate America, survival has become a global struggle. Many firms are beginning to make room for innovators by giving managers the freedom and incentive to create and market their own ideas.

While creative challenge is indeed the case in some forward-thinking companies, it is not the reality for the majority who work in management jobs. Yet your chances for success in working for *any* company will be enhanced if you possess entrepreneurial traits. The entrepreneur's instinct will identify you as a mover and a shaker rather than a manager who is simply good at the job.

However much you may enjoy your career as you rise through the ranks, seeds of discomfort can grow. You may continue to have a strong desire to be free from the constraints of the company. Through the action of honest self-appraisal, most executives are familiar with this sense of discontent in some form or another; but it is uncommon to experience it to a degree that would motivate you to sacrifice your job, especially if you're in a management position.

Many assume that the desire to be in business must be powerful enough to make a complete break with a job seem like a viable option. The truth is that it's simply too much to expect for those whose entire working life has been devoted to working for someone else. Even for those who have already become sort-of entrepreneurs by becoming franchisees, reluctance remains to break the ties with a parent franchisor in order to become completely independent of the parent company.

This was demonstrated some years ago when Winchell's Donuts offered to rescind the franchise agreement of some 600 franchisees. They were given the option either to get their franchise investment back and leave the chain—and thus become free to go out entirely on their own—or to rescind their franchise agreements in order to join the company as employees.

Only a handful opted to go on their own and the rest, en masse, became employees of the company. Even after having learned how to run their stores as franchisees, they had no desire to be in business *all by themselves.* Full-time entrepreneurship is simply unacceptable to most people.

The problem is that to remain unsatisfied in your job will only lead to lifelong disappointment by suppressing your desire to be your own boss; to resign from your job will put you in limbo. You would have neither the security of a job nor a proven, alternative way of making a living. In my own case, once I had established myself in New York in a management position, I decided to take the plunge. I resigned in order to return to California to start a full-time business.

My friends were convinced that I had lost my mind and in the clear perspective of hindsight, I must confess that it was not a smart move. Why did I commit this admittedly imprudent act? It was not undertaken thoughtlessly; I had mulled it over for at least a year. My quitting was justified by the same reasons so many others have used. As foolish as what I did may seem, it's done all the time and usually for the following reasons:

- We *assume* that there will be a conflict of interest between our job and a moonlight business.
- We are fearful of not being able to handle both.
- We do not even consider the alternative of a moonlight business (as was my case).
- There is a rule ingrained in our minds that we must be either an employee or an employer, but not both.
- There may be geographical considerations, such as my desire to relocate in a business far away from where my job was located.

Entrepreneurs go into business to satisfy an instinctive need to be independent as well as to be successful. But no matter what your preconceived notion might be regarding starting with a completely clean slate, make your decision without any bias other than the determination to improve your present position. Focus your thinking completely on putting more grain into your storeroom, and not taking out any that you have stored up.

Stop and think: why *should* you give up what you already have (a job) in order to achieve the rewards of starting a business? This is not a quid pro quo situation, "an equal exchange or substitution." Having a job is a treasure chest of points toward winning the game of achieving security. And to win in any game, do not give points away.

If a machine is beyond repair, then it makes sense to scrap it and start over. Look at your job in the same light. Most jobs are not utterly beyond repair. Quite the contrary: they're our basic source of income. If yours is hopelessly unrewarding, then you should replace it with another, so that your career is still preserved as an ongoing source of security.

The primary career should remain a basic building block in your overall plan for accomplishing financial independence, unless the moonlight activity grows enough to make it truly redundant. Since American culture already accepts people working in moonlight jobs, it will also accept an ethically structured moonlight business as well.

There is yet another reason why it is an imprudent step to resign your job. You may have enough money to be financially independent for a couple of years while you decide on what business to get into (as in my own case). Not having any assured income will leave you with an increasing anxiety to do *something*. The nest egg that grants you the time to think is also the source of capital for starting up your business. The more time you take to look around, the less capital you will have to start up. This urgency makes it all the more difficult to calmly look into all possibilities.

When I resigned, I found myself without any means of support, which is not a very stable springboard from which to plan a future. If you start out under the protective income of a job, you won't make the kind of mistakes that grow out of the do-or-die approach. As it was, I made things much more difficult for myself than was necessary.

By quitting my job, I traded all that I had built up in a secure career to satisfy my desire to be in business. I was willing to risk everything to accomplish this. Take it from me, this is really not a good idea. There is another, more preferable alternative; if you really want to quit your job, then have a proven business lined up and operating first, and then quit.

So which is better—to become a moonlight entrepreneur or to quit your job altogether in order to start a business? By now the answer should be quite clear. I made the mistake of resigning from my job because I didn't know better, but there is no need for you to do likewise. The bottom line is not to quit your job at all, no matter where you are on the corporate ladder or where you are living and working. Start out as a part-time entrepreneur instead, in that marvelous, independent, moonlight world.

# CHAPTER SEVEN

# Think for Yourself

It's no secret by now that I am an advocate of moonlighting, or that I believe it doesn't matter whether economic forecasts are good or bad for you to be successful. All you need to do is think for yourself and avoid making some common mistakes. Yet, to be fair, there are two sides to every issue and therefore we should also consider the arguments *against* becoming a moonlighter. The following opinions by my devil's advocates can be summed up under the (borrowed) heading, "Surely You're Joking, Mr. Holland!"

**Devil's Advocate Number One:** You say that I should prepare for hard times by starting a business on the side. For the sake of argument, I will admit that my job is not as secure as it was in the past. But the reason I haven't started a business is that I'm unwilling to gamble my future by taking on that kind of risk, which everybody knows is frightfully high. Businesses go broke in bad times, especially start-up ones. So if times do get tough, the safest plan for me is to concentrate on my job and avoid moonlighting like the plague.

**Devil's Advocate Number Two:** First I am told I can't count on my job. Next I'm told that the solution is to start a sideline business. Then I'm persuaded that this might result in a conflict of interest which could cost me my job. C'mon, gimme a break!!

**Devil's Advocate Number Three:** My position, precarious as it may be, is going to be made even riskier by moonlighting, because I would have to hold down my job and at the same time divert my attention to starting a business. To become more secure, should I not take *fewer* risks rather than to intentionally take on new ones?

A central question emerges from all this: is it possible to become more secure by taking on *more risks*? The answer depends on the kind of risks you take. Some you can control, and others will be controlled by outside forces. If the risks are entirely within your own power to control, then the results will be the direct outcome of your own actions.

If the risks you incur are influenced by what happens on the "outside", including the accuracy of someone's predictions, then factors *beyond* your control will determine your destiny. The risk you take in buying a common stock is one that you cannot entirely control. Its value will go up or down, and your success will depend on whatever inscrutable market forces are at work on the stock. This certainly will not depend on how well you perform, other than in your initial judgment in making the buy. The prospective moonlighter should separate risks into three categories:

▸ Risks you can control completely by yourself
▸ Risks you can control, but which are subject to outside forces playing a contributing role
▸ Risks you have no control over whatsoever.

Keeping in mind that there's no cast-iron insurance, the question is to what degree other people or events can influence the outcome of the venture. Playing chess is a game in which the outcome depends entirely upon the individual player. There is no luck apart from getting black and white pieces. But if you go to Las Vegas to play blackjack, you must accept playing against the house odds. If you decide to gamble a hundred dollars (and no more), then you are still fully in charge as to the extent of your possible losses. You have put a cap on your risk.

In self-controlled risks, your own personal skills become the determining factors; whether it's gambling or starting a business, you can limit your exposure to loss. The moonlighter's game is to control whatever risks you choose to take (which will be covered in Chapter 8, Limit Your Liability) and make sure that success will depend on what *you* do, rather than the fall of the dice.

There are other risks in which you surrender partial control because external forces can influence the outcome. It's the difference between playing golf and baseball. Taking on a business partner, for example, brings an outside force into play. A partnership may indeed add the factor necessary for success, but from the point of view of risk-taking, the outcome is now partially out of your hands.

Consider the worst possible approach for the moonlighter. It's entirely possible to go about a business venture and unwittingly surrender all authority to influence its outcome. When you approach *everything* imprudently, then the risk is total and everything becomes a matter of sheer luck. If you start a business without a regular job, without experience in the business, and without a cap on liability, the probability of loss becomes so great as to become unacceptable. It's no longer risk taking but becomes a game of Russian roulette.

The selection of *what* business to start is critical, and this decision is one you will hopefully make with extreme care. If your intended business does well during hard times, your future is not going to be impacted much by outside economic events. In fact, some do very well indeed during bad times. I know, because I was once in such a business, which happened to be doughnuts. (People stop eating steak and eggs for breakfast and instead eat more doughnuts to save money.)

But there are a multitude of similar business opportunities that will prosper during hard times. Maybe you won't buy a house during a recession, but you will fix up the one you have—and the business of remodeling begins to flourish. You can't get your oil changed in service stations any longer, which has created ten-minute oil-change shops. When times get tough, these places will do even better. Within your own field of interest, there may be all kinds of recession-proof opportunities.

As well, the thinking moonlighter does not expose all the family assets to wipeout, but instead chooses just how much to risk and restricts the risk to this sum and not a penny more! Thus, the successful moonlighter can take *on* risks in order to achieve security. Sure, we will risk failure, but only in a calculated and limited way.

You will definitely not risk your job—your fallback. And it's within your own power to eliminate potential conflict of interest arising between your job and your business. You either create conflicts of interest or step around them; it is entirely up to you.

Any start-up, like birth, will have dangers that are inherent in the traumas of coming into being. After start-up, there are later phases, such as major expansion or diversification, which will also be inherently risky. But the reason most people fail in business is that they make fatal mistakes that are unrelated to external factors. It is *human error* that so outrageously increases business failures.

It is said that the restaurant business is the most risky of all. Indeed it is, because so many restaurateurs make such atrocious mistakes in opening them. I once failed in a restaurant business because I naively delegated the operation to those who were (so-called) experts. Thinking for yourself includes avoiding this kind of mistake by gaining experience in a business that interests you (working for someone else already in it) before striking out on your own.

The final answer to our chorus of devil's advocates is that you need not accept the economist's gloomy forecasts at all. Experts have a penchant for proclaiming what the future holds because so many of us wait with baited breath for what they have to say. We depend on their advice to make risk-taking decisions, some of which can be enormous in scope. These financial gurus can always justify their predictions of the future by carefully selecting other events that they accurately predicted in the past.

What they fail to remind us is that many of their past predictions went expensively wrong. The events that experts are so confidently predicting as you read this can be upset by other events that have been overlooked in their forecasts. A special niche is reserved for the precious metal gurus, who dogmatically tell us what the future holds for gold and silver. Again, they will justify their credentials by pointing to some past success, without mentioning mistakes that made rich widows go back to work as waitresses.

Who knows the future? Nobody knows. We only can be sure that unanticipated, quite simple events will confuse the most erudite of experts. The rule I recommend for moonlighting is to think for yourself. Rely instead on the basics you believe in.

Consider the rule followed by J. Paul Getty: Purchase things when everybody else is selling, and sell them when everybody else is buying. He didn't have to predict future events at all; high is high and low is low, because in the first case everyone is buying and in the second, everyone is selling.

Assuming your sideline business will fulfill needs in hard times, does the plan to become a moonlighter cease to be worthwhile if, instead, the nation enjoys prosperity? Of course not. It is just possible that the United States will emerge into a bountiful period of its history; that budgets will be balanced, productivity will soar, and world trade will flourish. If such good times do materialize, then *all the better for the moonlighter.*

Your moonlighting plans need not be fueled by fear of catastrophe, nor by high hopes of prosperity, nor by predictions of the future. Come rain or shine, what matters is to think for yourself and to limit risks to those that you control. By observing these rules, your success will depend not so much on outside forces but on how you go about it. And best of all, your working life will no longer be a spectator sport.

# CHAPTER EIGHT

# Limit Your Liability

$P$laying it safe is the essence of moonlighting. While you should be prudent about hanging onto your job, through zeal or inexperience you can become ensnared in unacceptable obligations. You might wake up to realize you're risking more money in the venture than was ever intended. And, more often than not, you will find *all* of your assets in jeopardy.

To prevent this, you must follow a strictly disciplined plan that we will call "Limit Your Liability." For instance, a creditor may demand a personal guarantee. The difficulty is that a personal guarantee puts virtually all of your net worth at stake. This is something about which you want to think more than twice.

In medieval England, people were constantly at risk from foreign invaders and bandits who would swoop down and ravage everything in sight. To protect against these raids, the inhabitants built stone towers. When threatened, they would retreat into these fortress-like shelters where they could hole up and protect their lives, if nothing else. These towers still remain as evidence of how those resourceful people defended themselves against surprise attacks.

My kind of moonlighter goes into business knowing that there are going to be risks, but at the same time ensuring they are limited ones. You need the protection of a fortress to guard against your creditors. They will attempt to extract every form of security possible in order to improve their chances of profiting from your inexperience.

You can build a tower to insulate yourself from unacceptable liabilities. Start your moonlighting with a predetermined maximum amount of money that you are willing to lose, and vow never to be at risk for an aggregate amount which exceeds this sum.

Let's assume that you have a job, as well as total savings of $100,000. Let's also assume that you are willing to risk $30,000 on a moonlight business. Your situation is not entirely unlike the predicament of those English townspeople: creditors are going to come along and want the security of every one of those hundred thousand dollars.

The first step in preparing your defense is to identify each potential enemy. Once you have identified these threats, you can build an effective structure, block by block, to protect your financial integrity. The moonlighter's entire net worth can become exposed to risk by the following:

- ▸ Personal guarantees
- ▸ A long-term lease
- ▸ Working capital needs that exceed start-up limits
- ▸ Personal liability for business-related lawsuits
- ▸ Excessive inventories
- ▸ Slow-pay or bad receivables
- ▸ Uninsured losses

Keep in mind that a direct hit in any of these areas can precipitate a hemorrhage of dollars. When this happens, your financial net worth is going to bleed until there's not a drop left. Not a single exception can be permitted in adhering to the following safeguards. The idea is to isolate certain assets from risk—principally your job, but also that part of your net worth you wish to leave at home rather than bring to the entrepreneurial gaming table.

Uncapped personal guarantees are the greatest threat to the moonlighter because in the event of failure, everything goes down. I speak with authority on this subject, because a long time ago there was an unhappy episode in my career when everything I had worked for was swept away. It is pertinent here to explain the reasons why I went under:

- ▸ I started a business that I knew nothing about: a chain of franchised Mexican restaurants. I should have learned about the business by working in it first.
- ▸ I expanded it far too fast.
- ▸ I signed unlimited personal guarantees.

I haven't signed an uncapped personal guarantee since that horrible episode, other than to banks. The only reason that banks remain an exception is that they are inflexible on this point. With others, I have insisted on limited guarantees. Your lenders, creditors, and landlord will all ask for your personal guarantee. If you agree at all, you must be prepared to negotiate some mitigating clauses.

If you start as a proprietorship, you are automatically going to be personally liable for the obligations of your business. This is the first reason to form a corporation; it, and not you, becomes the entity that is obligated. Now you will *surely* be presented with personal guarantee forms to sign! They are written in legal jargon and will give you a headache to read, but you can be sure they will expose all of your personal assets in the event of default.

To make matters worse, some bankers will ask for a secondary mortgage on your home so that if you don't pay them, your home can also be taken in a simple process of real estate foreclosure. I didn't purchase my present home from the previous occupant; I purchased it from a bank that had foreclosed on some unfortunate borrower who had gone into default on a commercial loan. Do not put up your home as security for anyone, including banks. You are giving the lender profitable business; they are not doing you a favor. And if a bank demands a mortgage on your home, find another bank.

You can't deal with all creditors without offering some personal guarantees, but there are rules to follow when you do. First, explain to them that you're starting out as a moonlighter and have agreed with your family not to jeopardize unrelated assets. If your creditors are adamant, then insist on a limited form of guarantee. Suppliers, after all, have much to gain in writing new business, and they will be willing to undertake risks in the interest of making money.

Creditors will normally agree to a stipulation that the guarantee becomes void after the business has gained a certain net worth. It is, therefore, an interim guarantee that is waived once your company has proven itself. For a business starting with a total investment of $30,000, I would say that $30,000 would be an amount to try for as the net worth at which the guarantee is nullified.

Your lease will have a very large potential liability. For example, if you rent a space for $1,000 per month for five years, your obligation is a total of $60,000. If your maximum exposure is supposed to be $30,000, by signing *one agreement* you already have incurred a single liability that is twice the total you intended.

Landlords have as their main objective filling up vacant space, and they will be reasonable in considering a limited guarantee. I never had a landlord find this limitation unacceptable. Furthermore, your lease must be modified in two other ways to reduce your liability:

- Insist on the right to sublease to another business.
- Sign a short-term lease with long-term options.

Your lease must provide you with the right to sublease the premises for another use. And it *must be stated* that approval "will not be unreasonably withheld." This becomes critically important if your business isn't working out. You will still be liable for the rent, but will hopefully have a subtenant offsetting your own obligation.

Also, you will want assurance that your location will be available at an agreed rent over a reasonably long period of time. The simple—but imprudent—solution is to sign a long-term lease. The problem is that this obligation may be greater than you are willing to risk.

The solution is to sign a very short-term lease, with periodic options that cover a much longer term. For example, sign a one-year lease with two five-year options. During the first year you can determine whether you wish to continue on, and if so, exercise the first five-year option. The risk of the five-year option period is acceptable because the business has now become seasoned.

The next step in limiting your liability will require you to be completely familiar with cash-flow planning. A sure way to lose control of how much is at risk is not knowing how much money the operation is going to take. You get started only to find that more and more must be committed, until finally everything is in jeopardy. The worst eventuality would be to discover that more cash is required than you're able to raise. Now you're up in the air in a flimsy plane that has run out of gas.

If you do not know how to forecast your cash flow, my advice is to go back to school (night school if necessary) and acquire this knowledge before going any further. How can you expect to win in a game when you can't keep score? Before you even start, your cash-flow projection is going to disclose the total investment required, including when and how much you will need to borrow.

Your liability must be foreseen by long-term cash-flow planning *before* you start. This is a simple technique that will tell you in advance the total cash required. Very simply, it involves plotting all sources of income, together with all the ways that money is to be spent. This can be done on a monthly basis over a long period of time (say, a year). By carrying forward the cash balances each month (starting cash, plus income, less expenses), a picture quickly emerges that will tell you not only how much but also when cash is required.

Another risk is exposure to personal liability in lawsuits. We have become a suit-happy society, fueled onward by juries awarding enormous damages. You must therefore protect yourself against lawsuits. The basic defense is to do business as a corporation. You will need a good lawyer anyway; the first issue on your checklist should be the pros and cons of forming a corporation. Your corporation will become the entity at risk, rather than your entire personal estate. But while this will insulate you against personal liability, there are ongoing costs and taxes for corporations that must also be considered.

You will also need a good insurance agent. I would suggest seeking out one who routinely handles a good deal of business insurance and who has multiple sources from which to place the coverage you will need. It is vital to have adequate insurance for catastrophic losses. Your agent may recommend additional umbrella coverage for your casualty policy. In some businesses, high insurance rates have prompted owners to carry on without being covered, which violates our "Limit Your Liability" code in spades! It's not a matter to take lightly.

Another way to limit your liability is to maintain a practice of buying from hand to mouth when starting up. All too often, the desire to buy at lower unit costs will compel the beginner to purchase larger quantities than are really needed. This may work for seasoned businesses having the experience of knowing how fast merchandise turns over. Yet the start-up moonlighter goes into business with a limited amount of capital and ignorant of what rate of turnover to expect. Both are good reasons to avoid large purchases. While this practice is going to limit your liability, it will also help you avoid mistakes in purchasing. You won't believe how fast inventory can diminish in value because of obsolescence or style changes. Don't overburden yourself with it.

Let me give an example. When I first went into business, I manufactured automated bakery equipment. A partner and I made machines that were a maze of sprockets, gears, and bicycle chains. My partner would buy a half dozen sprockets when the machine in production needed only one. His reason was the usual "economy of scale" argument: the price per sprocket was less when we bought six of them at a time, and "we will always have a use for them." Hah! We nearly went broke because of all those extra parts. Had we not sold the company to Pillsbury, we could have opened a chain of hardware stores.

Obsolescence can occur overnight in the present age of lightning-fast changes in technology. Heaven help the computer store entrepreneur who doesn't buy from hand to mouth. The fax machine purchased today will inevitably be displaced by a cheaper, more versatile, and higher-capacity model next month. And that model will be displaced the month following. Whether it is food, fashion, or shoes, a conservative buying policy is going to help you keep within your guidelines of liability.

Another way to limit your liability is to establish a conservative credit policy before you start. After you have made your start-up investment, your only source of cash will be the money received from customers. If your customers are slow to pay or don't pay at all, your whole investment will be at risk. Slow-paying customers increase your liability by requiring you to inject more capital, because a cash-flow projection cannot maintain equilibrium with bad debts. You might consider the following in setting your credit policy:

- ▸ If you are going to extend credit, have each customer checked out with a credit reporting facility. Your banker will help you.
- ▸ Deal with your customers and vendors in written terms. Use forms that spell out your credit policy and describe exactly the nature of what is being sold or purchased. Don't depend on a firm handshake—not out

of mistrust, but because we simply do not remember things that are not spelled out clearly.

- ▸ If you're selling special-order merchandise, require a sufficient deposit to insure yourself against loss in the event the customer cancels.
- ▸ Don't give excessively extended terms in order to get business; this may come later when your business is seasoned.
- ▸ Don't hesitate to deal with customers on a COD-only basis.
- ▸ If it is appropriate to sell your merchandise on a purchase contract, sell the contract to a finance company or to your bank. Trying to be a banker on an installment sale will kill your cash flow.

A conservative credit policy is going to eliminate customers who want better terms than your policy allows. The consolation in this is that the policy weeds out customers that you can't afford anyway. Saying "no" will gain the respect of your customers; it should become the single most important word in your credit vocabulary.

The final item on the "Limit your Liability" checklist is to control uninsured losses. I am not referring here to possible defects in your insurance coverage. I am addressing the kind of uninsured losses which can destroy your profit. They are called *shrinkage* and *employee theft*.

Sorry folks, but welcome to the fallen world of business. While an all-cash operation has marvelous cash flow benefits, there is the rather delicate problem created when every sale is made: does the sales clerk ring the sale up, or is the money pocketed? A large supermarket in Palm Springs just closed its doors because of shrinkage; it could not control shoplifting during the surges of holiday crowds.

The way to learn what sort of problems to expect in your own business is to go to work for the most successful competitor and let them teach you. If you're going into the grocery business and want to learn all about shrinkage, get a job at a 7-Eleven. This education will be well worth your trouble. Each business has its own specialized assortment of losses, as well as safeguards. Using this knowledge to draft an appropriate cash control system for your employees will prevent your business from bleeding to death.

The overall goal of limiting your liability is to prevent financial exposure beyond your initial intentions. If your obligations later become greater than anticipated, any additional investment above that ceiling becomes a decision for later on. If your initial plan is to risk $30,000, then as long as your cash flow requirements and personal guarantees do not exceed that amount, you have stayed within the "Limit Your Liability" fortress.

Each of the items we have covered in this chapter should be considered a brick in that fortress. Each must be in place in order to preserve your limited liability. The mortar holding all of this together is discipline, which is unfortunately not always a natural virtue in us entrepreneurs.

But remember that the moonlighter is a special breed of entrepreneur: one guided by prudence, not one inclined to risk everything on a single throw of the dice. Going into a moonlight business should also be fun. And the comfort of knowing that it's not going to be a do-or-die matter will greatly enhance the prospects of it being so.

# CHAPTER NINE

# Everybody's Doing It

I n this chapter you will find out about moonlighting from the point of view of those who have already made the plunge. What motivates people to become moonlighters? Do they have any common characteristics? Most important, what can we learn from their mistakes? Their stories will teach some "how-to" lessons and at the same time turn your entrepreneurial furnace up higher.

New opportunities are opening up in hundreds of fields. Businesses are not getting bigger (as we were told so often they would) but are instead getting smaller. More and more, small companies are running rings around big companies. Moonlighters are not burdened by expensive overhead, archaic policies, or high-priced and unproductive help. You can zero in on one target with deadly accuracy and enjoy the benefits of specialization. Large companies, for all their economic strength, find this increasingly difficult to compete with.

There is impressive statistical evidence to support the claim that moonlighters are entering a period of greater opportunity. *The Handbook of Small Business Data: 1988*, a product of the Office of Advocacy of the U.S. Small Business Administration, shows where national employment trends are heading. The greatest growth in employment is taking place in the smallest firms; the largest firms are showing the smallest gains. From 1980 to 1986, employment grew 27 percent in firms under twenty employees while employment grew only nine percent in firms with more than five hundred employees.

Not all of us have the good fortune to be motivated enough to moonlight—to *seize upon opportunity*. The following moonlight entrepreneurs took that stand. All have certain common characteristics:

- ▸ All but one are actual persons in actual moonlight business.
- ▸ They all are people I know.
- ▸ All have full-time jobs in addition to being successful moonlighters.
- ▸ There is a lesson to be learned in each of them.

▼

| | |
|---:|:---|
| NAME: | Terry Haney |
| JOB: | Business Consultant |
| MOONLIGHT BUSINESS: | Furniture Refinishing |

Paradoxically, Terry's regular job is being in business for himself! Before starting his moonlight venture, he demonstrated an entrepreneurial zeal far exceeding that required of a moonlighter: he resigned his job at Systems Development Corporation after spending twenty successful years with the firm. Operating his own consulting firm, Temjam Corporation, he now works long hours, dealing with state and local governments.

In his spare time he always enjoyed his hobby of refinishing old furniture, so he decided to start a second, and this time, moonlight business. He rented a 1,500-square-foot warehouse and took on a disabled friend whom he trained to do the refinishing. Terry then began making (deductible) trips to England and Ireland to purchase antique furniture at bargain prices. He shipped the pieces back by the container-load, refinished them, and conducted sales out of his warehouse/factory/showroom.

By word of mouth, people throughout San Fernando Valley learned about his business, and he began refinishing items of furniture that customers brought in. During a period of three years, two things happened: Both his consulting business and his moonlight refinishing business grew by leaps and bounds.

Finally, Terry had to decide which one to concentrate on and which to give up. Reluctantly, he phased out the moonlight venture. Under other circumstances, he could have expanded it into a full-time business. We learn from Terry that the exploitation of a hobby (that fills a need) can become a marvelous opportunity for moonlighting.

| | |
|---:|:---|
| NAME: | Al Croce |
| JOB: | Aspiring Actor |
| MOONLIGHT BUSINESS: | Wood Deco Ducks |

Al's decision to become a moonlighter was born out of pure, sheer hunger. He went to New York intending to enter the world of legitimate theater. As actors do, he holed himself up in a cold-water flat in Greenwich Village, a grungy fifth-floor walk-up. During a period of two years he went to acting school and made all the traditional (and heartbreaking) efforts to make it in the theater. Just about the time his meager savings had dwindled to zero, he finally got a bit part in an off-Broadway play, yet he still couldn't make enough money to keep a roof over his head.

Finally, out of desperation, Al and another unemployed actor (both of whom were adept at working with their hands) began carving wooden ducks to sell on Fifth Avenue street corners. These flying ducks had brass wings and were the sort of ornaments that might look good over a fireplace. Well, there are lots of fireplaces in New York, and Al's ducks began selling!

The more they turned out, the greater the demand grew. They finally started a factory. The last time I saw my friend, he was still interested in the theater but no longer as a starving actor. He was driving a Mercedes, had a garden apartment on Ninth Avenue (with real grass), and had satisfied his love of Broadway by regularly attending all the season's hit plays! Al became a moonlighter out of the basic survival instinct; it became his ticket to entrepreneurial riches.

|  | |
|---|---|
| NAME: | Rosario Jiminez |
| JOB: | Cement Foreman |
| MOONLIGHT BUSINESS: | Avocado "Retailer" |

Rosario is now retired, but for twenty-five years he worked for Robert McKee Company, a large contracting firm. Rosario was laid up for an extended period of time because of an accident, and his savings were finally used up. Out of sheer physical need (as was the case with Al Croce) and too proud to accept charity, Rosario began canvassing door to door, selling the avocados that grew on the trees in his back yard.

This moonlight activity sustained him until he was able to return to his regular job. If you ever lose the regular income from your job, remember that moonlighting provides a means for survival when all else has failed. Rosario didn't need the stimulus of entrepreneurial instinct. He was motivated by an empty cupboard and a hungry family.

|  | |
|---|---|
| NAME: | Tod Silvers |
| JOB: | Airline Clerk |
| MOONLIGHT BUSINESS: | Mail-Order Credit Cards |

Tod is now thirty-three years old and is well on his way to financial independence. He was a reservations clerk at Western Airlines when he started to moonlight. While his job provided him with an adequate

**49**

HOW

income and free trips to Hawaii, his new-found wealth comes from an insatiable entrepreneurial appetite.

His first moonlight activity was in the mail-order business. He advertises for customers in those newspapers you buy (or peek a look at) at the checkout stand in the supermarket. His classified ads are targeted to those who, for any number of reasons, cannot obtain credit cards. Tod's business is to obtain "plastic" for these customers.

It has become an enormous success, to the extent that a second moonlight activity has emerged out of the necessity to invest the money he made from the first! His newest undertaking is to buy apartment buildings; his goal is to own enough units to become truly independent. When his job disappeared because of an airline merger, moonlight activities became his parachute to safety.

How could anyone have picked up such unusual business expertise? He claims he had simply read about it in a book that explained everything he needed to know. He then merely followed the instructions! This explanation was made plausible to me later when I came across Entrepreneur Magazine's catalog, "267 New Ways To Make Money." (Their telephone number is 1-800-421-2300.) Some of the suggested businesses included newsletter publishing, pet cemeteries, cookie shops, automotive detailing . . . and so on, to a total of 267!

Tod's business also highlights how effective mail order can be for moonlighting. It doesn't require the office, the hours, or the employees you must deal with in a more traditional business. And the possibilities of mail order have expanded because of 800 telephone numbers and credit cards. Similarly, when television began to be utilized as the advertising medium, telemarketing was born and is still growing. The merchandising of products and services via these methods will be covered in more detail in a later chapter.

|  | |
| --- | --- |
| NAME: | Ron Evans |
| JOB: | Telephone Engineer |
| MOONLIGHT BUSINESS: | Retail Fish Market |

Ron worked for Southern Bell for five years as an electrical engineer. His restless energy, however, was inadequately harnessed by his job at the telephone company. To vent his entrepreneurial urge, he decided to exploit an invention of his—an ingenious metal rack designed to keep firewood dry when stored on the humid soil of northern Louisiana. The rack could be telescoped in or out to handle different sized stacks of wood. It also kept the wood off the ground, which allowed air to circulate around the logs.

Ron started to build his stackers in a small garage along the roadside in his home town of Bossier City. He set up a small display of the finished product in front of the shop and, sure enough, found that there were customers for his product. This humble beginning turned Ron's entrepreneurial furnace up higher, and he began looking for another moonlight activity.

He noticed that an increasing number of customers at the local meat market were asking for fish, a demand stimulated by the widely publicized benefits of a low-fat diet. As it happened, Ron had been making trips to southern Louisiana to purchase crawfish, first for his family and then, increasingly, for his circle of friends. He could buy these "mudbugs" for ten cents per pound, yet as "crawfish" they were selling in local markets for the same price as good cuts of meat.

His entrepreneurial juices were flowing now, and he had learned that you don't need a complex business to succeed as a moonlighter. Instead, it seemed to Ron that all he had to do was *one* thing, and do it well. He added a fish stand alongside his display of firewood stackers, and began selling crawfish at a dollar a pound. He was soon deluged with customers, and quickly expanded his venture by adding shrimp and redfish.

Finally, his stand blossomed into a full-fledged market specializing in all kinds of fresh fish. For more affluent customers, he added varieties of very expensive fish that he paid a high price for, and therefore didn't provide the same high margin of profit. His biggest business came from low-income customers to whom he sells in high volume at better profit margins. Ron finally purchased two acres of commercial land along the highway and built a combination fish restaurant and market. It has become a huge operation—so successful that he finally quit his regular career at the telephone company.

His transformation from employee to full-time entrepreneur came about because of his inner compulsion to take that first step, small as it was. And that first step bore little relation to what he finally settled upon as his biggest money-maker. Marketing the wood rack resulted in a journey into a quite different opportunity that he seized upon with gusto. His achievements grew out of—*starting.*

|  |  |
|---|---|
| NAME: | Debbie Rady |
| JOB: | Fire Department Clerk |
| MOONLIGHT BUSINESS: | Real Estate Sales |

Debbie's story as a moonlighter could be an example for thousands of women who share the same circumstances. She is divorced and has the responsibility of raising a thirteen-year-old son. Her salary at the fire department doesn't permit her many of the good things in life, including the prospect of a college education for her son. Nor does her job give her the opportunity to meet people on a social basis. Her future promised little more than dreary work and a reclusive existence.

Out of some spark of entrepreneurial determination, she decided to do something beyond her job to bring some zest into her life. She was also determined to make the extra money she needed. Debbie studied for and passed the real estate salesperson's test, and went to work part-time for a real estate broker, selling houses in her community.

Job conflict is not a concern for her, because her activities in real estate are clearly unrelated to her job. Debbie has met her goals of making more money and enjoying a new, more interesting life.

|  |  |
|---|---|
| NAME: | Chuck Johnson |
| JOB: | Controller, Sunkist Growers |
| MOONLIGHT BUSINESS: | Deco Nails |

Chuck's story is an example of how an artistic hobby can turn into an unexpected source of moonlight income. His hobby was to create pictures by pounding nails of various sizes and shapes, which form intricate designs, into wooden blocks. In the evenings, he found relaxation in this activity; over a period of time, he accumulated more of these pieces than could possibly hang in his home or be given away to friends.

Chuck finally decided to go commercial. He began displaying his work in the art festivals held in local parks, and now conducts an ongoing business in these shows, selling his pieces to enthusiastic buyers who find them unique as well as artistically appealing.

Once again, an amateur interest or skill can become a profitable source of moonlighting. When we work at something we enjoy, it becomes a pleasure rather than work. Making money doing what you love doing is not a bad idea at all.

|  |  |
|---|---|
| NAME: | Suzie Wrong (fictitious) |
| JOB: | Secretary |
| MOONLIGHT BUSINESS: | Manuscript Service |

Suzie works at a university as a secretary to two top professors. Much of her work at the university is done on a DEC word processor.

Suzie's moonlight business is preparing manuscripts for authors. Her clients are secured by advertisements that she places in *Writer's Digest* Magazine; her services are sold on a per-page basis. She also has a word processor of her own at home that is compatible with the one at the university—so far, not bad. The additional income is certainly welcome to her, and she has become a high-speed expert in this field.

Unfortunately, she has not been discreet in separating her regular work and her moonlighting activities. She engages in the moonlighting business while she is at work. I suppose when opportunity is present (in her case, having free time on her job), the inclination to keep busy can lure us into the tar pit called "conflict of interest." And perhaps the climate of academia is more forgiving than the business world, since most academics are moonlighters themselves!

Regardless of her work environment, however, Suzie is violating a basic principle of moonlighting. Her job could be put in jeopardy by this practice. On the positive side, she is doing what she does best and if she can contrive to keep the moonlight activity apart from her job, she may well enjoy both job and business.

|  |  |
|---|---|
| NAME: | Dave Murray |
| JOB: | EDP Technician |
| MOONLIGHT BUSINESS: | Amway Salesman |

Dave is included in our mix of moonlighters to determine whether part-time commission selling should be considered entrepreneurial moonlighting. Part-time commission selling includes activities such as real estate, insurance (A.L. Williams has now passed Prudential), and direct sellers such as Avon. Over the years, Dave became an enthusiast of the Amway system and its line of products. His Amway selling doesn't conflict with his job, since it is conducted during the evenings and on weekends.

The direct-selling companies of this country have done an outstanding job in promoting an evangelical fervor in their salesforces to go out and sell, sell, sell! I would suggest that direct selling may not be cut out of *quite* the same cloth as starting a self-run business.

Yet this form of moonlighting is nonetheless commendable; it is an expression of entrepreneurial zeal that could be expanded later into a truly independent business. For instance, moonlighters in real estate sales can become full-fledged brokers: true entrepreneurs in anyone's book. So let's not be disdainful of those who seek out these selling opportunities in order to enter in the moonlight world!

NAME: Phil Holland
JOB: (Former) Business Co-owner
MOONLIGHT BUSINESS: Commercial Developer

I find fun and profit in developing small commercial shopping centers. Until the spring of 1989, when I sold out my interest in Yum Yum Donut Shops, I moonlighted while working as co-chairman of the firm. My partner, Frank Watase, and I had an agreement allowing each of us freedom to do projects on our own, keeping in mind that everything we did would be communicated to the other partner.

My last moonlight project while still co-chairman was a small shopping center in San Bernardino, California. The original site consisted of a drive-up Kentucky Fried Chicken unit that was built off a corner property, leaving vacant land on the corner. I purchased the property from the KFC franchisee in a sale-leaseback deal and then built out a new 3,000-square-foot retail building on the corner, which is now leased to a chain of furniture stores.

This moonlight endeavor did not occupy a great deal of my time, because I hired an experienced real estate broker to handle both the acquisition of the property and the leasing of the new building. I retained an architect who specialized in designing small projects, and then hired an experienced builder to construct it.

My incentive to moonlight in real estate, aside from the profit potential (always a strong motivater), was to exercise my entrepreneurial inclinations in a sphere wholly independent from my job. My wife, Peggy, also participates in this business by handling the property management functions and keeping the accounting records. Her incentive is to satisfy a desire to be active in a worthwhile activity.

Both of us, in our different ways, have reasons to moonlight. And now that I am out of Yum Yum, the ongoing development of shopping centers will provide me with a prideful reason to say "I'm in real estate," rather than confess my true occupation, which is being a full-time tennis bum.

▲

All of the moonlighters I've mentioned have the common trait of being endowed with high energy levels. There is, therefore, something to be said in favor of going for it while you are young rather than in the latter stages of your career, when youthful stamina has flagged somewhat. Some of these moonlighters were motivated by a specific need, such as raising money to live on when jobs had been lost or could not be found. Others were simply fulfilling a desire to try out an idea. Once the initial project is embarked on, an entirely new confidence takes over that propels the moonlighter into other, and usually bigger, endeavors.

All of them were motivated by financial reward and the satisfaction gained from self-directed efforts. Most were surprised that things turned out so well, once they gained enough courage to start. All of them overcame their fear of taking the first step, that scary chasm separating the entrepreneur from the "not quite yet" individual.

Whether fighting for survival or exploiting an idea, all of the successful moonlighters made it by zeroing in on a product or service that filled a market need. Was it worthwhile for those who did? In most cases, the rewards far outweighed the regrets. For those whose first undertaking was a flop, they nonetheless had crossed the most difficult hurdle of all, getting started.

There are lessons to be learned from examining how others go about moonlighting. In the examples here, we have picked up the following:

- ► Almost anybody can do it.
- ► There is a vast range of possibilities for everybody.
- ► Those who make the plunge tend to get into what they are good at and what they enjoy doing.
- ► Three words that kill success in moonlighting are "not right now." The winners are willing to take that first step, *right now*.
- ► A great deal (if not everything) hinges on selecting the right business.

You could list your own moonlighting examples all day. In fact, you should do so in order to learn how good or bad decisions affected the moonlighters you have known personally. Ask yourself: how much does the moonlighter have to lose, provided that a good job is not impacted and enough prudence is present to limit ultimate liability? For yourself, the greatest question may be what line to get into. I hope you have the good fortune of the moonlighters cited here: to get into something you're good at or love doing, or best of all, both.

One approach I do not strongly recommend is that of Al Croce, whose success grew out of starvation. Or Rosario, whose loss of a job forced him into the streets, shouting "Avocados for sale!" When you undertake moonlighting, do so from the security of a job. Then it becomes an adventure rather than a do-or-die, eat-or-starve stand for survival.

# PART THREE ▼ WHERE

Certain kinds of businesses are especially appropriate for moonlighting. You can retrieve the ones you're interested in by reviewing the chapter headings. Use these ideas as springboards to develop possibilities of your own.

# CHAPTER TEN

# Picking the Right Moonlight Business

I now invite you to sample one of the more delectable aspects of moonlighting: namely, deciding on what to do. You should abandon for the moment any preconceived notions, because you may discover possibilities you previously would not be caught dead doing. Your imagination should be in the hang-loose mode because you're not looking at business opportunities in the clear light of day, but in the subdued glow of moonlight.

As a moonlighter, you don't have complete freedom of movement, because of the limitations imposed by your regular line of work. My recommendations are therefore going to have a clear bias in favor of moonlighting, as opposed to businesses that require full-time commitment.

Sometimes choices can be made automatically by preestablished goals or existing know-how (for example, Mrs. Field's Cookies). More often, choosing a business is an agonizing and elusive process. It shouldn't be; there are simply too many delightful possibilities. Yet the choice is not to be taken lightly. Your success will largely depend on what business you select. This will be the most important decision of your entrepreneurial career. The following considerations should all be factored into your decision:

- ▸ Is it truly a growth opportunity?
- ▸ Can I enlist the support of others to carry it off?
- ▸ Will it conflict with my job?
- ▸ Will it be fun to do?
- ▸ Do I have the necessary expertise to pull it off?
- ▸ Does it fall within the limits of what I am willing to risk?

The importance of timing should also be considered, as some businesses are in growth and others in decline. John Naisbitt's *Megatrends* became the principal source of buzzwords for describing and listing growth situations, which Naisbitt refers as "sunrise" opportunities; he describes the declining segments of the economy as "sunset" businesses. I would concur that having an overall sense of growth trends is all to the good. There would be no point in hitching your wagon up to a vanishing star. Who in their right mind would want to open up a tobacco store or watch repair shop today?

Nor do opportunities all fall within easily drawn definitions. Pursuing sunrise buzzwords doesn't always work. Let's combine three of them: retailing, service, and computers. You might expect that this package would be a sure-fire success as a business selection. Not necessarily, because in the past two years, hundreds of computer retailers have been the victims of overconfidence, inability to keep abreast of innovation, or simply a downturn in business. It doesn't always follow that you can win in a business just because it is categorized as a "growth situation."

The moonlighter who depends entirely on a shopping list of sunrise opportunities may miss other, more rewarding ones under his or her very nose. For example, an interesting trend is emerging in garage-shop firms. A growing number of blue-collar entrepreneurs are starting very ordinary businesses. In an article entitled "Starting Up," Bill Richards of the *Wall Street Journal* reported that small business start-ups now include a surprising quantity of these blue-collar participants. Nearly ten percent of displaced blue-collar workers who have returned to work are operating their own businesses! They are going into fields that connect with the kind of work they formerly did.

Three laid-off employees of International Harvester Company, a foreman and two welders, now operate as Admiral Improvement, Inc. Their first order was to clean and renovate production machinery for Tenneco, which, to cut costs, stepped up the amount of work farmed out to independent contractors. They are doing what they are already good at, in their own business.

My favorite example of a sunset business is one that is labor intensive. The moonlighter doesn't need the increasingly complex problems of dealing with labor, nor the competition from offshore competitors who can undersell him. Yet not everything is made by people. Shoes are, and dresses are, but not everything. If your product can be made by a machine, then as an American moonlighter you can compete with anybody in the world.

The United States is the right place for the entrepreneur interested in marketing a product that automatic machines can turn out. If this is what you have in mind, you're fortunate to be in hog heaven. You can utilize the biggest market, up-to-the-minute technology, the finest designers, the best communications and means of transportation, and your own merchandising know-how. Does it take a sophisticated business school training to avail yourself of this potential? Not at all.

You will be among the first to know about a product now in development that will put all of these typically American qualities into play. The moonlighter behind this project intends to make it big through the development of this single product. She believes that it will have a widespread demand because it answers a need that is unfilled in her own household.

The product won't bear the legend, "Made in Taiwan"; it will be designed, produced, and marketed right here in the United States. Not to keep you in suspense, it is a decorator-designed squeegee to wipe down the shower door, incorporating a wall-hung holder and a decorative plastic handle. (So how did you wipe down *your* shower door this morning?)

This is in fact my wife Peggy's current moonlight venture! Someone with lower costs won't deter her, because the product is going to be made on automatic extrusion machines right here in California. Not that it's easy; it takes research and testing, trial and error, and some up-front money to get it launched in the market place. And you can do the same with any product of your own imagining that fills a widespread need.

In some of the growth segments mentioned in *Megatrends*, there are dangerous cross currents as well as pockets of disaster that may cause problems for the moonlighter:

| Growth Area | Problem |
|---|---|
| Health care | Cutbacks in Medicare squeezing hospitals and care centers |
| Nutrition and fitness | Hard times for some health-theme restaurants and American-made sports equipment |
| Leisure | Not always a recession-proof business |
| Retailing | Some time-management problems here for moonlighters, and new competition from discounters |
| Technicians | Probably the pick of the bunch for the moonlighter |
| Law/accounting | May indeed be good territory for the moonlighter |

This is not to say that Naisbitt's generalizations are not on the whole valid; they are. But there will be both flourishing and declining opportunities in *any* field. At the present time some forms of commercial real estate, especially office buildings and shopping centers, are oversaturated. Yet, other types of real estate, more appropriate for the moonlighter, are thriving. This second category includes low-cost housing, fixer-uppers, and all aspects of financing. Also keep in mind that a troubled real estate market will provide marvelous opportunities to purchase distressed properties from highly motivated sellers. Tomorrow this may all change and be quite the reverse; you must be correct as to timing as well as to choice of activity.

My role in presenting moonlight opportunities to you will be that of a maître d'. I have no idea what moonlighting dishes you prefer, and can only present you with entrées I happen to like. You should expand the menu to include ideas of your own. Your selection could be an application of your present know-how, or it could be something you could learn about and then practice (such as studying to become a real estate agent). It could be to fill a personal need that has troubled you; then determine whether your idea can become a business format that will satisfy the needs of other people.

To fulfill your inner (and perhaps never expressed) desires may call for your becoming a giant in your field, or it may call for setting up a business to polish shoes. *Don't let pride get in your way.* The most humble business can be enormously satisfying. An unpretentious operation can gratify basic needs not only during periods of prosperity but during recessions as well, and also has the potential of becoming a large business for people who are inclined to grow and grow.

Just as a moonlight exercise, let's explore the humble activity just cited to see what kind of an opportunity it might offer: the possibility of shining shoes. For years, I have experienced difficulty in having this menial task performed. I am too busy (and lazy) to go back to doing it myself. Yet I have this nagging, ongoing upset, because my shoes are never what I'd like them to be, and I never know where to take them. I would pay at least $2 to get a good shoe shine and would be happy to take four to six pairs at a time to have them done.

Now, if a moonlighter started this as a sideline business and built it to twenty such customers a day, five days a week, the sales would be $50,000 a year. Operating costs would be very low. And if it were *me*, I'd hire and train inexpensive labor on some kind of piecework basis. Also, wouldn't it be fun to conduct a catchy advertising campaign to promote this service? (Perhaps a trial offer: Bring one shoe in and get the other one shined for free!)

I would then acquire one of those compact machines that replaces heels in five minutes, and offer this service as well. To really get things going, I'd display a limited line of informal shoes, or perhaps gift items, or greeting cards, or . . . do you get the idea of the entrepreneurial mind at work? That $50,000 could expand into $200,000 very quickly.

This brings us to the second step. Once you have the initial idea, look carefully into whether it makes any sense as a business. As it happens, I have no idea whether shining shoes does or does not. I use it only as an example to illustrate that opportunity may well lie in humble pursuits. Whether shining shoes makes sense as a business would depend on how much rent you will have to pay, how long it takes to shine a pair of shoes, how much the polish will cost, how much you will have to pay employees, and so on. Can you field test it first in a small way? (I hope so, because how else are these matters to be determined?) The point is that a great idea must also pencil out.

There are many opportunities to do a better job than the established players—to fill needs of a higher order than simply getting shoes shined. Wherever there is inadequacy, there is opportunity. Simon Geller runs an FM radio station out of his apartment in Gloucester, Massachusetts. He has created a niche from which he cannot be dislodged, all because he says less than any other broadcaster in America. He has succeeded as a commercial operation by airing listener-supported commercials of between three to six minutes of advertising a day.

Don't limit your range to what is listed here. Remember to look for opportunities close—really close—at hand. Here is a summary of opportunities (to be discussed at length in the following chapters) that are especially ripe for moonlighting.

| Moonlighting Opportunity | Why |
| --- | --- |
| Market a single product | Your time is limited, so concentrate everything on a singular objective. |
| The hollow corporation | New horizons beckon aspiring tycoons to compete with the biggest of 'em. |
| Real estate | You'll find big bucks, big leverage, and it's definitely not nine to five. |
| Food | If this book had a cover picture, it would be that of a man or woman, in a kitchen, making cheesecake. |
| Direct marketing | The benefits are manifold: no hourly restraints, no rent, no overhead. You can utilize marvelous new communication tools: plastic credit and the 800 number. |
| Serve people | Needs are expanding, and new ones are emerging. |
| Privatization | Privatization by governmental agencies and subcontracting by private industry are on the march. |
| Family opportunities | Moonlighters need support, and where better than within the family unit? |

Let's first look at some potential hazards. Traps are to be found even in the most inviting business opportunity. For one thing, today's opportunity can become tomorrow's overcrowded jungle quite abruptly. The natural business rhythm of sunrise/sunset is indeed the very reality of life; it's all a matter of timing. The wheel keeps turning, and what is at the top today may well be at the bottom tomorrow.

I don't think that all moonlighters need to go into franchise deals. In spite of the initial attractions, the reality of many of these business relationships becomes an entirely different matter. They can be high in front-end fees and start-up costs and very dear in continuation fees (extracted as you go along). They will also restrict your freedom to do as you please (one of the original reasons to become a moonlighter) and could demand more time than you have available. If a franchise deal doesn't work out, in many cases it's the franchisee who gets burned; the franchisor will simply sell the turkey to someone else.

For moonlighters who go into a food operation, emphasis must be placed on just what food to select—not only from the standpoint of what is good to eat but also from the point of view of what is *good for you* to eat. We now know, through well-publicized mountains of research, that we actually will live longer and healthier if we avoid certain foods and eat more of others.

It would be prudent for the moonlighter to give ample thought to this new awareness. Your potential customers are picking up on all of these new facts, just as you are. There is no doubt that in the future dieting and exercise will become American lifestyles. You should not place emphasis on marketing foods that are continually identified on television as carcinogenic or contributing to the likelihood of heart disease, stroke, and so on.

For example, I don't think it would be a good idea to go into the egg business today. Given the choice between going into the fish business or the sausage business, I think you could work out which one to select. And if I had to do it all over, I'm not sure that I would go into doughnuts at all. (Heaven help a doughnut shop today that doesn't also sell baked goods.)

Moonlighters interested in manufacturing a product must obviously factor in the high cost of American labor. This problem can upset the most hopeful of plans. For example, one of the great sunrise opportunities of the past decade has been jogging equipment, but stark contrasts can be found between the stories of those who first entered the field.

Nike is the classic example of astounding success; but keep in mind that virtually all of their products have been made in offshore factories. Other producers in the same business experienced crippling difficulties. Van Shoe Company, every bit as successful with respect to timing, became a disaster story because they could not compete. All of their products were made in their American factories, and they finally had to file Chapter

11. Van Shoe is now coming back to life again, but will no longer be producing all of their own shoes.

Some American companies *are* beginning to learn how to compete against imports. General Electric's share of the dishwasher market has climbed to 41 percent (from 28 percent in 1982) because they made drastic assembly line changes and more fully automated their aging Louisville plant. GE's gains in productivity have cut the time it takes to build a machine from three days to eight hours. They also found new ways to lower material costs. For example, the interiors of their dishwashers are no longer expensive enameled metal, but are made entirely out of plastic.

Outboard Marine now sells outboard motors that are less costly than Japanese imports because of a six-year exercise in progressive cost reduction. They started with a complete overhaul of the company that entailed shutting down enormous plants and having component parts made and assembled in smaller, more efficient shops. So there *is* hope for moonlighters who want to put that red, white, and blue USA label on their merchandise.

Breathtaking changes are occurring in retailing. Discount chains with sales up to 100 million dollars per outlet per year deal in razor-thin profit margins. These "category-killers," operating out of enormous warehouses, play havoc with traditional retailers. Twenty three percent of ALL toys sold in the United States now pass through the check-out stands of Toys'R'Us. You might now begin to understand the meaning of "category-killer."

The Price Club's 100,000-square-foot membership wholesale stores sell so cheap that other retail businesses are buying supplies from them. And Price Club clones are springing up all over America. Warehouse outlets now influence almost everything we buy including food, hardware, electronics, appliances, books, toys, and liquor. The moonlighter must accept the fact that customer loyalty is going to stop at the pocketbook.

This means that if you're planning to open a retail store, you must know whether your location and price structure can generate enough volume to survive such ruthless competition. For example, the traditional liquor store had better be prepared to depend more and more on convenience food sales.

There are no hard and fast (or easy) rules to distinguish between the good and the bad when it comes to selecting a moonlight business. The most promising opportunities today may not be so tomorrow. As Philip Anderson explains, "Yesterday's fad is today's relic and tomorrow's new style. Keep your wardrobe long enough and it will become fashionable again."

Forget the business opportunity columns in the newspaper, the franchise shows, and the business brokers. First and foremost, consider satisfying your own instincts. You have ample resources of your own to draw from. Ask yourself the following questions:

**Work**          What have you gained from your career that you would enjoy making into a business?

**Hobbies**       Do you have a hobby that can become a moonlight business?

**Education**     Do you have any specific know-how that you would enjoy doing on the side, as a business?

**Family**        What would the family like to do together?

**Pleasure**      What could you do as a moonlighter that would give you a great deal of fun and satisfaction?

**Fill a need**   Is there a product or service missing in your life that others would buy?

I will confess that if I had used this approach at the very outset of my entrepreneurial career, rather than feverishly scratching in the business opportunity columns, I would have done a great deal better. Back then, I was going crazy, looking everywhere to find that perfect opportunity. And I neglected to spend enough thought on what I would really *like* to do.

I did have one idea of my very own, which was to start a pie shop. I had an aunt who was an expert pie baker. She would have been delighted to show me how and even make the first pies. *Pies?* I thought. It would be great fun and an interesting business but, c'mon, I wanted a *real* business. And so I got into one that I knew nothing about, completely foreign to my background and nothing whatever in the way of fun. This all happened in 1964, the same year that Marie Callander started her pie shop. She sold Marie Callander Pies in 1986 for 90 million dollars. So, if you have your heart set on an idea and can do it better than anyone else, then consider it *very* carefully.

What we all are seeking is a magic ticket for success. I recently appeared on a television show to talk about start-up businesses and received a letter from a viewer. It was from a lady who had started a moonlight business, "Tiffany's Original New York Cheesecake." She wrote: "I started two years ago and it hasn't been easy. I lease oven time in a bakery but I'm unable to find another place to bake or get more time where I am. And I have so many opportunities to grow. Restaurants call me and I have to tell them I'm unable to supply them. I stopped promoting because nine out of ten times I get the account. If there is a secret to success, I'd love to know about it."

This lady may not fully appreciate it, but she is already experiencing the secret of success: she is doing something she loves and is good at. And she cannot produce enough to satisfy eager customers. Sure, it's not easy; she'll run into an assortment of growth problems, and solving these is going to take a great deal of hard work. At the present time she is stymied, but so long as her determination remains steady and her quality remains consistent, she's going to become successful in a bigger way.

For her, the process of selection came easily. She missed good New York cheesecake, was unable to find it, and knew in her heart that she could fill this gap. She experimented with a basic recipe that originated from her mother's Jewish heritage and was perfected by her father's Italian background. She knew that by fulfilling the demand for really good (that is, currently unavailable) cheesecake, she could sell them. That is all it takes to pick out a business. Draw up this example: What can you do uncommonly well, which will also bring satisfaction to customers? That, in essence, is what moonlight selection is all about.

I would suggest that you test your ideas against the list of factors given at the beginning of this chapter on page 59. When you come upon the idea that sets you on fire and therefore passes the test, you should experience an excitement that will drive you onward. You'll exude the entrepreneur's glow, and your mind will shift into overdrive to plan how to do it.

We now are going into my moonlighter's menu in more detail. This may spark the idea for your business. Keep in mind that there are more than 240 million people out there in the U.S. and more than 5 billion throughout the world. And "if a man . . . make a better mousetrap than his neighbor, tho' he build his house in the woods, the world will make a beaten path to his door." Emerson's advice reinforces what is so especially appropriate for the moonlighter: having a unique, singular, competitive product or service. There is a very big world out there to buy it.

# CHAPTER ELEVEN

# The Single-Product Solution

$M$oonlighting gets its name from the time during which the activity usually takes place: night. If you can keep it that way, your chances for success will improve greatly. You have a limited amount of time for moonlighting, and all too often running a sideline business can become uncomfortably demanding. This problem becomes simplified if you're only dealing with one item; I call this the "single-product solution."

This approach is also more acceptable to your employer. Most employers are going to have *some* concern about employee moonlighting. Your interest in a widget is not going to create the same level of apprehension in your boss as will your leaving the office at the end of the day to go to your restaurant. Stop and think: if the tables were turned and *you* were the boss, wouldn't you think twice about your employees having their minds on another job? Since the single-product solution will help keep your moonlighting activity relatively uncomplicated, it deserves special attention.

There is a second and even stronger reason for considering the single-product approach to moonlighting: businesses that specialize do better than those that do not. Dedication to a single product will inevitably result in a higher level of competence. If your only interest is in *one* product, you are going to know it backwards and forwards. The specialist will know more about the product than the non-specialist, which leaves the non-specialist at a disadvantage.

If you doubt this, consider this example. I recently had surgery on my elbow. If it had been *your* elbow, would you have gone to a general surgeon or to a specialist? I chose to see an orthopedic surgeon with a good reputation in sports-related medicine. He can do seeming miracles because his practice is limited to surgery on elbows and shoulders. How could a general surgeon do those operations as expertly? The same is true in business. When you want an ice cream cone, where do you go?

A single-product business can also grow unbelievably large. Even the most seemingly unimportant idea can become an enormous enterprise. If it satisfies a widespread need, there will be thousands, perhaps millions of customers to sell to.

The single-product approach also suits the majority of start-up entrepreneurs. People are motivated into starting a business more by the desire to exploit an idea than merely the wish to be in business. During a radio interview on the Larry King show, I was invited to answer questions about how to start a business. Calls began pouring in from all over the country that took me completely by surprise. I was amazed to discover that people were not so much interested in the how-to aspects as they were in asking, "What do you think of this great idea of mine?"

To summarize, the single-product solution rests on these four cornerstones:

▸ A relatively uncomplicated moonlight business lowers the risk of conflict of interest with your regular job.
▸ Specialists do better than non-specialists.
▸ A single-product business can grow to be much larger than a "regular" business.
▸ More of us have specific ideas rather than businesses in mind.

But how do you get that idea in the first place? *What* single product, you may ask. Some of you may already have ideas to begin with. But let's assume you are starting from scratch. The first step is to eliminate negative thinking; no idea is too small or silly. The solution to a seemingly insignificant problem can result in astonishing success.

Some years ago, a man had chronic trouble with the wire connection to his hearing aid; it kept breaking. He had no experience in miniature technology, but he did know that he was not the only one with this difficulty. He finally decided to invent a better connection on his own, which not only solved his hearing aid problem but others' as well. This was the start of Microdot, Inc., which ultimately became a New York Stock Exchange company specializing in miniature aerospace connectors.

The process of discovery starts with the question, "Why not?" Do you have any unsatisfied personal needs? The first place to search is close to home. Ask yourself: What single product would fill a widespread need (and not conflict with my job)?

Let's suppose you enjoy jogging. Once you're into it, you become familiar with the gear that jogging requires. If *I* were to devise a product for runners, it would be an inexpensive pulse meter that could be used while running. The main objective in aerobic exercise is to elevate the pulse to a certain level over a prolonged period of time. While this is *possible* to measure while running, it's not easy.

Your family and friends are sources for single-product ideas. Ask them the following questions: "What is your pet peeve? What product would be a good idea for me to develop?" At some point, the bulb is going to flash, and you will have discovered the product that you can begin to develop. Expect the unexpected to occur.

Sometimes unusual ideas will open up new horizons. Whoever develops the joggers' pulse meter will soon discover that the device will be in demand for other sports activities as well. On the other hand, the idea may not work out for the purpose intended, but instead may serve another one.

When Ray Kroc first traveled from Chicago to visit the McDonald brothers' hamburger stand in San Bernardino, he didn't go with the intention of starting a nationwide chain. He was just very curious as to why they used so many malted milk machines. (At the time, he was in business selling these units.) What he saw opened up entirely new vistas for him. He dropped the malt machine business, and began the fantastic story of McDonalds.

Not everything is going to fit neatly into little boxes. Work with the pieces available to you, even though they don't all fit together. Eventually you will begin to develop those elements that work, and learn to discard those that don't.

It will help you to visualize the solution. Picture the product in your mind and what it will do. Peggy's interest in the squeegee was nurtured because she knew precisely what it would look like. She can foresee the potential buyer coming upon her product in the store. In turn, the buyer is going to picture the product at use in the bathroom and will be motivated to buy because it will solve a nagging problem. Visualizing the solution will also help you anticipate hitches and give you direction in working out difficulties.

Follow your own hunches before following the advice of others. Peggy took her squeegee to an industrial designer, whose visualization of the proper design did not match her idea at all. When you're involved in a single product, your intuition will be reinforced by the cumulative expertise you've built up in that one field. You will have greater confidence in your own decisions and will begin to depend less on the opinions of others.

This is not to say that you shouldn't sometimes take on the characteristics of a large sponge and soak up as much as possible from others in the know. Their opinions may correct your own thinking in case you have been approaching your project from the wrong direction.

I am not a great believer in inventing new wheels. Too often a product is so unique that nobody is interested in it. The world doesn't need new ways to do things as much as *better* ways to do them. The greatest opportunities lie in solving existing needs better than before, with more attractive, easier to use, and less expensive products. My idea for a runners' pulse meter is not a new one. There are such devices on the market now, but they are clumsy and expensive.

Once you have your idea in hand, the first step is to develop a prototype. Your first visit should be to a print shop—to get some business cards made. (Your lawyer will tell you how to go about getting your business name properly recorded.) Now you have the credibility of being in business, rather than someone with a harebrained notion. When Peggy makes a call to Goodyear Tires, they send samples to "Green Isle Development Company." She is accepted as a potential customer and enjoys the quiet satisfaction of being her own boss—already.

If your product is truly unique, talk to a patent lawyer before talking to an industrial designer. Patent attorneys deal with new products every day; they can give you advice extending far beyond merely legal issues. Your patent attorney can answer questions such as: Is it appropriate to deal with an industrial designer at all? What would be a reasonable fee to pay? How can you get assurance of confidentiality before disclosing ideas to designers? What alternative avenues of development are possible?

Before dealing with patent lawyers, industrial designers, or vendors, be sure to have a clear understanding of how fees are to be charged. Don't give on-the-spot approval of any proposal involving money. Sometimes we go along with a proposition because we want to be agreeable, or we're in a hurry, or we wish to gain the approval of those who are pitching us. Crucial decisions are best made *after* meetings, when you can coolly scrutinize the issues without the pressure of matching wits with someone. It is much better to say, "I'll think about it and get back to you." Then shop around.

Most start-up entrepreneurs with new ideas are usually nervous about someone stealing it and beating us to the marketplace. While this is always possible, you can take comfort in the fact that usually it doesn't happen for a number of reasons. First, there is a great chasm between having an idea and having the fortitude and capital to carry it off. The person who can do this is a rare breed. Also, what may seem as a great idea to you may not be so captivating to others. It's normally safe to ask questions of people who are in a position to give you well-qualified opinions about your idea. This would include potential buyers as well as those who may be your vendors.

An industrial designer may be required to take your idea to the prototype stage. If so, talk to a number of them. The first consultation is usually free, but make sure of this beforehand. Some products are so technical in nature that outside help is definitely going to be needed. In these instances, industrial designers can become so expensive that unless you have deep pockets, they can zap your bank account long before you have the prototype.

You would not believe how much money can be spent in the early stages of a simple project. One reason is that designers like to charge by the hour, and you don't want to pay by the hour. Have your patent attorney approve the contract, because you will need agreement on issues such as confidentiality and patent or trademark rights.

A successful developmental entrepreneur must possess the ability to glean necessary information from others, and especially from experts in unfamiliar fields. Who knows better than potential vendors? You can give suppliers the requirements on a need-to-know basis, without their even knowing what your other plans might be. They can tell you what works and what doesn't work. Preconceived ideas that are not checked out by this kind of research can lead to (easily avoidable) disappointment.

One book will open up a world of help: the Yellow Pages. This resource will grant you access to people with specific knowledge who are motivated to assist you because they want to become your suppliers. If you live in a large metropolitan area, you're going to find many sources for your components.

The smart moonlighter will cultivate the burrowing power of a go-pher to root out information from the specialists who have already gone through the trial-and-error process. If Peggy contacts half a dozen rubber companies (all from the Yellow Pages) to make extrusions for her squeegee, she will soon get an expert and balanced view of what is going on.

And since she only has a single product to deal with, she can examine every possibility to learn proven solutions from those who have previously dealt with the same problems. She can call the purchasing departments of firms already making squeegees and find out from whom they buy their rubber. Could you extract this fact with one long distance telephone call? It would be great fun trying and would take a bit of imagination as well. And by managing to locate their sources, you would have gained access to their knowledge.

It's going to take more time—and more money—to develop a single product than you will at first imagine. An initial estimate of three months will probably turn out to be a year. The $400 for the model may run up to $5,000 by the time you have a prototype ready for market testing. Complex electromechanical or electronic products can take millions of dollars to get going, and are rarely appropriate products for the start-up entrepreneur. You *could* grow old or go broke trying.

Here is a summary of some things to keep in mind when developing a single product:

- Do business as a company.
- If appropriate, first talk with a patent attorney.
- Get first visit (complimentary) advice from a number of industrial designers.
- If your product is genuinely unique, have an agreement of confidentiality drawn up with those whom you consult.
- Have a handmade prototype made.

72

- ► Use the Yellow Pages to learn from vendors.
- ► Remember that style will distinguish and sell your product.
- ► Test market a small (but necessarily expensive) production run first.
- ► The more people you talk to, the more you avoid mistakes—so talk.
- ► Evaluate production opportunities overseas.
- ► Learn the merchandising avenues for your product.

In many cases, the product can be designed and made by yourself. Many of the largest businesses were started in garages, and if not in garages, then in kitchens. You're not limited to just cheesecake or cookies; *anything* that you can do well becomes a prospect for your single product.

Gail Ganus had some reason to feel insecure. She was experiencing the frustrations of most of those who seek careers in the theater. Especially troublesome was the difficulty she had in making enough money to make ends meet. When Gail was a baby, her father had opened a restaurant that still does business, specializing in barbecued ribs. While growing up, she spent a great deal of time in the restaurant, where she learned (of course) how to make her father's special barbecue sauce. Do you see a single product idea emerging here?

Gail became a successful moonlighter in her kitchen; she started making "Gail's Hot and Sassy Barbecue Sauce." Before starting out, she tested every competing brand of sauce on the market. She didn't have to rely on any outside advice about how to put together her product because she *knew* she had something special; it had been refined for years by her father.

Equally important, she had a flair for merchandising and an unquenchable drive for success. She called Gelson's Markets, a chain of nine upscale supermarkets in southern California. The buyer consistently refused to see her on the grounds that they didn't have the shelf space for yet another barbecue sauce.

With the true zeal of a moonlighter, Gail prepared a hot, sizzling platter of ribs, drenched in her barbecue sauce. Without an appointment, she walked into the store and with a flourish presented this aromatic feast to the buyer. The result was an initial order of five cases per store.

A single-product moonlight business was born. Gail didn't need any consultants (excluding her father), and it all started in her kitchen. If her business is to grow, she will have to face the new challenge of having her product made under her own label by a qualified vendor. But the first step had been successfully taken.

Sometimes inner zeal can blind you to the outside world's desire (or rather, lack of desire) for your product. It may not fly. I remember one retired tycoon who spent $75,000 developing a kite, only to find that no one would buy it. He still has a warehouse full of them. This kind of mistake may sound improbable, but it happens frequently because you can become so enamored of an idea that you lose a cool sense of objectivity.

**73**

There was no question that the kite entrepreneur believed in the kite; his mistake was to assume everyone else would share his enthusiasm. My kind of moonlighter would have market tested it first. Had he manufactured only a hundred of them, he would have learned soon enough that the world didn't share his fascination.

And it is so easy to test the idea first. It may cost $400 to make up a handmade squeegee, but by doing so all kinds of valuable lessons can be learned: how it works, how it catches the eye. The prototype then becomes the model for the drawings needed by the molder. You can show it to department store buyers to get their opinions.

Even after this phase, if all is still "go," hold off going into full production. Regardless of the production cost per unit, first make a handful for market testing. It is wiser to produce 1,000 units and sell them at *no* profit than to make 100,000, only to find a previously unnoticed design flaw. This approach will limit your risk as you go.

When you think about it, most opportunities of the moonlight variety are indeed single products: One item, done spectacularly well. And this applies to any field of business. Let's use real estate as an example. Real estate has become segmented into all sorts of specialties:

► Commercial:  1. Shopping centers

　　　　　　　  2. Office buildings

　　　　　　　  3. Industrial

► Residential:  1. Condominiums

　　　　　　　  2. Single family houses (tracts)

　　　　　　　  3. Single family houses (individual)

　　　　　　　  4. Remodeling

　　　　　　　  5. Rehabilitation

Each of the above specialties are further divided into smaller specialties, such as brokerage, leasing, and management. The moonlighter who is considering real estate had better stop and think of the amount and degree of competition in this field. This is a highly specialized business today. Even within the field of shopping centers there are smaller subdivisions, each requiring different expertise:

Strip centers:　　100,000-square-foot neighborhood centers, with a supermarket as the key tenant

Enclosed malls:　The big leagues

Mini-centers:　　The convenience store corners

Let's look at a single real estate specialty, mini-centers. In California, La Mancha Development Company has put up *hundreds* of these, and they are only one of dozens of companies who specialize in this field. (And no matter *what* your product is, you are going to come up against somebody like La Mancha.) In their specialty, they know precisely how much to pay for the land—but you don't. They know what the tenants will pay to the last cent and what lease terms can be extracted to the last concession—but you don't. You are going into the ring with the world champion in that particular class, and this will happen in any field you enter.

The solution is to decide what *specialty* (single product, if you will) to pursue, and learn how to become a champion in that particular class. The problem for the novice moonlighter is that the specialists have already made all of the mistakes—and learned from them. And there are lots of mistakes to be made: in design, in architects, in tenant mix, in lease negotiation; setting up your business can become a snake pit of risks. If everyone were working with the same degree of experience as you, the moonlighter, then the playing field could be level. But to survive you must play as an expert yourself.

One burial ground for real estate developers could be called "Condominium Hill." I know contractors who have made fortunes in their own specialty, only to crash in flames because of the allure of building condominiums. We *think* we know all about houses because we live in them. If you are interested in moonlighting in real estate, my advice is to first look over the whole field, and then pick out a highly specialized niche. The problem in *not* following this "single product" approach is that if you try to do it all, you will be zapped by the specialists.

Specialists also excel in professions and services. It is easy enough to understand that if I need to have my elbow fixed, I'd rather have an orthopedic specialist perform the operation than a general surgeon. And it should be equally clear that when you sell your house, you're going to list it with the best residential specialist in the neighborhood. The same rule applies to every business that comes to mind. Would you hire even a gardener unless you were convinced you were hiring a pro?

Food is a field where specializing in a single product is a proven approach. At the county fair we line up before the stand that sells *only* hot dogs, and not the one having a long menu too small to read. It works like this everywhere. Another example could be taken from a flea market I visited in Rosarito Beach in Baja California. I was sightseeing one Saturday morning, and observed a throng milling about the dozens of stalls displaying all kinds of clothing, foods, and craftwork. But no one seemed to be doing much business. What really caught my eye was a swarm of people crowding around one spot in an open area.

It was a single-product food operation; the crew consisted of mother, father, and their eight-year-old son, all working at a furious pace. Their "store" contained only a butane-fired, round frying kettle and a small extruding machine that looked like a meat grinder. The family was selling churros, a pastry extruded into hot fat and then sprinkled with cinnamon sugar. This operation had more activity than all the other stalls for yards around. And a single product can be expanded into Frito-Lay if you have the drive to do it.

Here's a final suggestion. If you already have a business in mind, ask yourself if it can be simplified down to specialize in a single product. The common thread of those who have narrowed their sights down to one product is that they end up doing a better job at it. If you want to moonlight by writing TV scripts, you would probably do best by becoming an expert in one genre. Once you have the key to mastering that specialized story line, you can then operate like a cookie cutter: repeating over and over what you do best. It applies to TV scripts, to squeegees, to food, to services; *you* must decide what would be the single product to zero in on.

Most who set out to market a single product do not reach their objective. A runner, if determined enough, can train to run a marathon, but the entrepreneur cannot rely on mere training. It's more of an obsession that you need to drive through to completion.

What makes product development harder than a marathon is that *unexpected* hardships will arise, and many will accept defeat. Perhaps this is a good thing, because quitting or losing interest is a painless way of cutting costs. But those with the true entrepreneurial guts will not burn out or become demolished by setbacks. Do you have what it takes? Perseverance is the trait that will separate the real entrepreneur from the almost-but-not-quite entrepreneur.

# The Hollow Corporation

A merican firms that make products are losing out to hollow businesses that operate at lower costs by *not* making products. We are depending increasingly on subcontractors or foreign producers to manufacture our wares, and this is causing the loss of American jobs. In this chapter we shall investigate how you can exploit this unfortunate turn of events.

We are becoming a nation full of firms that design and distribute, but increasingly depend on foreign producers to manufacture. And moonlighters can operate as hollow corporations, just like the big names do. Not only can you farm out manufacturing, but also everything else, from packaging to billing your customers.

*Business Week* magazine, in a special report dated March 3, 1986, entitled "AND NOW, THE POST-INDUSTRIAL CORPORATION— It could farm out everything from manufacturing to billing" cited the example of Lewis Galoob Toys, Inc., with sales of $58 million. By traditional standards, they're hardly a company at all. The entire operation is run by 115 employees. Galoob farms out everything: manufacturing (to Hong King and China), packaging, creative design, engineering, and distribution. They don't even collect their accounts; receivables are sold to Commercial Credit Corp., a factoring company. As Robert Galoob put it, "our business is one of relationships."

Is this appropriate territory for the moonlight entrepreneur? You betcha.

In the past, to market a product meant becoming a manufacturer. This is no longer the case; you can function by subcontracting your manufacturing to whatever firms can produce it at the lowest cost. The hollow corporation is just what its name implies—empty, a shell. The moonlighter can go into the business of "making" something out of a spare bedroom.

Today we have facsimile transmission, computer data bases, efficient worldwide transportation, and global financial services. With these new resources, "hollowing" can become your format, even though in the past you'd never have given it a thought.

The hollow corporation implies, principally, the absence of manufacturing. But it also eliminates fixed costs such as those of supervisory management and investment in plants and equipment. Operating as a hollow corporation does not necessarily mean dealing with vendors in Hong Kong. You can subcontract your manufacturing and assembly to local firms as well. You can be in a moonlight widget business without having to start a factory to make them.

The advantages of eliminating labor have become so attractive that many businesses are switching to a contracting relationship with former employees. The work is then performed on a contracted, piecework, or franchised basis. Some company-operated chains can no longer operate smaller outlets profitably, and to survive they are beginning to franchise them to independent entrepreneurs. By stripping away the corporate layers of overhead and fringes, the franchisee can make money at the same level of sales at which companies were formerly beginning to lose their shirts. The franchisee also is more motivated to make money than a company-employed manager could ever be. I know from first-hand experience that this is happening today in the doughnut business.

The architect in charge of store planning left my former firm to become an independent architect. Both he and the company agreed it would be better for him to operate outside the firm than inside as part of the staff. There are advantages for both parties. For one thing, he is now free to do other work. On the firm's part, his work will be performed on a fixed-fee basis that will be directly charged to each specific project. There's no more overhead or paying him employee benefits. In the past when there was a logjam of work, the architect couldn't handle it all, and the company would suffer losses because of lagging projects. On the other hand, during slack times when there was not enough work, the fixed cost of retaining a staff expert was difficult to justify.

I expect this architect to double his income by working out of his home. In his new role as a professional entrepreneur, he will actually benefit from the hollowing of his job. But it will be up to him to make a success out of his new architectural practice.

Another example of hollowing is taking place in the one-day auto-painting business. The payroll labor has been stripped by subcontracting the painting on a piecework basis. The management now knows at the start of the day exactly what the overall cost of painting a car will be, and is no longer concerned with payroll, payroll taxes, and paying people whether there is work to be performed or not. This is how hollowing is taking place in all kinds of labor-intensive businesses.

Caterpillar has survived and is now flourishing by subcontracting castings and other parts to firms throughout the world. Honeywell buys the central "brain" for its biggest computer from the Japanese, and imports mainframes from Europe as finished products. It is not only blue collar jobs that are being exported to foreign countries but management functions and engineering skills as well. There are only three alternatives for those in a business today: hollow, reduce costs, or go out of business. The start-up moonlighter doesn't have to ponder these choices, because the first one is the automatic answer.

Many American businesses are losing their competitive edge because they have not sufficiently invested in equipment or automation. Yet the moonlighter doesn't face the ugly problem of investing in expensive labor-saving equipment; you are free to *start up* in the hollow mode. You can aim for a business that is hollow by its nature. Here are two examples in which hollowing has long been the rule.

General contracting is a hollow-type business, because virtually all of the work can be subcontracted to specialized trades. While most forms of general contracting may not suit the moonlighter (because of the difficulty of building in the moonlight), it shows how one person, out of the proverbial spare bedroom, can literally take on millions of dollars of work. General contractors have been doing it for years.

The garment business has been a hollow industry since the time of the nineteenth-century sweatshops. According to one dress maker in Los Angeles, virtually none of the clothes made in California are produced by the firms whose labels appear in them. The work is performed by contractors who are furnished the cut goods and quote on the basis of a fixed price per garment.

Some garment firms have "inside contractors" who operate on their premises and who take responsibility for all aspects of the labor. In most cases, however, the work is done by immigrants in small neighborhood shops who depend entirely upon piecework for their pay. In residential neighborhoods of Kowloon, designer jeans can be seen by the thousands in the sidewalk sewing factories.

Yet you don't need to travel 7,000 miles to find vendors. Tijuana, Ciudad Juarez, and other Mexican cities bordering the United States have become low-cost production centers for American corporations. Across the border from El Paso, there are thousands of Mexicans working in more than 600 assembly plants, producing everything from electronic components to clothing. Twenty years ago, this area was occupied by tumbleweeds.

The American companies availing themselves of this low-cost labor include household names such as RCA, GE, GTE, Honeywell, and Xerox. Some firms manufacture parts in the United States (on automated equipment), send them to a Mexican factory for assembly, and then return them to the United States for packaging. And the Mexican labor force is still looking for more work.

Any moonlighter who starts a manufacturing business must initially decide whether to subcontract or to manufacture in-house. If I were to market a product requiring a great deal of labor, I'd surely spend some time in Tijuana to learn firsthand about the possibilities. The success of your business could depend on making the right assessment.

Inevitably, in some cases the wrong choice is made. A group of moonlighters in Ohio banded together to manufacture a small earth loader. In this instance the market was not dominated by a Japanese equivalent but by an American product, Clark Equipment Company's "Bob Cat."

Now, this was no group of ordinary bozos. They were well-heeled top managers of large manufacturing firms who wanted to collaborate in a moonlight adventure. Their opportunity surfaced when Warner and Swasey Co. decided not to invade the "Bob Cat" market with a similar product. The moonlighters decided that this was their chance to do just that. They successfully negotiated the rights to manufacture the loader that Warner and Swasey had decided not to go ahead with.

They set up a factory to manufacture their new product, to be sold under the trade name, "Beaver." Ultimately, the venture failed because they could not successfully compete with Clark. Yet parts could have been made in Hong Kong, and Mexican workers would have been available to assemble the machines. They could have enjoyed a decided cost advantage over the "Bob Cat." These entrepreneurs simply did not take hollowing into consideration. Could they have operated as a hollow corporation? According to one of them, they might well have done so, but it was never considered as an alternative.

The food business (to be covered in Chapter 14) is also suitable for the hollow mode and can work to the benefit of the moonlighter. There are bountiful production facilities everywhere for the private labeling of food products. These purveyors find that private label deals are very profitable. This additional volume maximizes the utilization of production facilities that are already in place (and costing money to keep in place).

The firm I started, Yum Yum Donut Shops, Inc., operates a mix plant in which fully prepared bakery mixes are produced. These products are then shipped to company shops. The facility is fully automated and represents a high investment. But this department also custom blends mixes for outside customers, and this has become an enormous business. Since the plant is already in place and paid for, this supplemental business is profitable at relatively small profit margins. And Yum Yum customers (including moonlighters) are provided a low cost, reliable source of supply that would be impractical to duplicate on a start-up basis.

At some later time, after a moonlight business has grown, it might make sense to manufacture on your own. But for the start-up, the utilization of already existing production facilities is a sensible way to start. It's therefore not necessary and usually not feasible to go into manufacturing when moonlighting with a food product. The investment in automatic production and packaging equipment will not be justified.

To get a broader perspective of hollowing prospects, I now propose an admittedly unscientific but effective method for random sampling of businesses from the local Yellow Pages index. Let's see which are candidates for a hollow business:

| | |
|---|---|
| All-terrain vehicles | If I were selling them, I'd talk to Honda. If I were making them, I'd probably go broke, even hollowing. |
| Barbecue stands | *Definitely* go with subcontracting. |
| Cabinet makers | I would subcontract both the manufacture and the assembly. |
| Electric transformers | General Electric abandoned the large transformer business because of overseas competition. This is definitely a case in which subcontracting to overseas suppliers would be necessary. |
| Food products, dehydrated | A great opportunity would exist here for importers, or for utilizing imports as a source. |

I now suggest you determine how hollowing would work if you were to apply it to your *own* prospective moonlight business. You may find opportunities to do so. For example, I once was in a business that initially seemed unsuitable for hollowing. Yet with the benefit of hindsight, it now appears that hollowing could well have turned this marginally successful company into a more prosperous one.

The business in question manufactured automatic machinery to order for large wholesale bakeries. It was a fully equipped manufacturing operation, including facilities for sheet metal fabrication, structural framing, welding, and a machine shop. After all the components were made, the machines would then be assembled by workers from all departments.

As it turned out, the business was never adequately profitable, in spite of overall customer approval of its products. (Yet the line was good enough to induce Pillsbury to ultimately buy the company.) My problem was that no matter what level of production was achieved or what price we charged the customers, the insatiable overhead of the labor, the factory, and the equipment together with all the related costs just ate me up alive. And these costs rolled on relentlessly, whether I had orders or not. When backlog was down, everything slowed down. When it soared, we could not manufacture the machines fast enough.

Looking back now, having experienced how hollow corporations operate today, I believe *everything* that went into those machines could have subcontracted. The parts could have been made in specialized outside shops — shops which had other customers to help support the overhead, rent, and equipment required. Had I done so, all those ongoing and unpredictable expenses would have miraculously disppeared. The components could then have been put together like a huge erector set. I could have *fixed* the cost of the stainless steel hood, the structural frame, the welding, and virtually everything else, including the assembly. Also, I would have had more time to concentrate on sales rather than be tied down with factory management. The firm would have been on a far sounder financial footing.

If hollowing could work for a company such as this, it seems to me that it could work for almost any other business as well. Yet to run a company as a hollow operation will take different management skills than are required to run it as a factory.

I would have had to standardize (freeze) the design of the machines. The rule "if it ain't broke, don't fix it" would have become strictly enforced. Detailed plans and specifications would have to be prepared for each and every part in order to instruct the subcontractor exactly what to make. Standardization would have been a benefit, because we were prone to constantly tinker with designs.

In managing a hollow corporation, the art of negotiation and contract management becomes important. You become a deal maker rather than a component maker. A hollow corporation manager requires salesmanship skills to gain pricing concessions, needs to maintain quality control, and must ensure timely deliveries. It takes a high order of organizational aptitude to be sure that the critical elements of production, finance, and marketing work together as a smooth running unit.

If the product is made overseas, a knowledge of international trade and finance, including letters of credit, will be required. University extension classes have a wide assortment of courses available for those interested in exploiting international subcontracting possibilities. Yet all of these activities can be conducted out of that proverbial spare bedroom. If you're a typical moonlighter, you will probably be more interested in exercising *these* skills than the kind required to run a factory.

In summary, the moonlighter can gain the following benefits from operating as a hollow corporation:

- There's no initial investment in factory, equipment, and running costs.
- You'll use others' expertise and technology.
- You'll exercise your communication and negotiating skills.
- Starting on a short term basis is OK; if it doesn't work, bail out.
- It's fast moving.

- There are no hassles with labor.
- You can get a fix on manufacturing costs.

In the past, American firms have stressed something quite the opposite to hollowing: namely, vertical integration. Henry Ford was clearly a pioneer in this method and went so far as to make his own steel, starting with the iron ore. If you can produce a product in-house for less than can be purchased on the outside, more power to you. It's now *you* who have the competitive edge.

The hollow corporation does have its drawbacks. Subcontractors can—and often will—let you down, and not always in a small way. Beech-nut Nutrition Corp., the baby food company, was horrified to have the U.S. Justice Department show up at their front door with indictments for the managing officers. The company was found to be selling baby food labeled "apple juice" that analysis had revealed to be flavored sugar water. Their (inadequate) defense was that "our supplier misled us." This obviously would not have happened if Beech-nut had been manufacturing the product in their own plant. The disadvantages of hollowed operations are:

- Imperfect quality control
- Potential competition from your supplier
- Alienation of design and manufacturing expertise
- Possibly higher cost of subcontracted manufacturing
- Less dependability of supply

Yet the more you consider a hollow corporation, the more you will turn up exciting opportunities. Be alert to the signals. Is it labor intensive? Can it be produced offshore? Does it have the potential of large volume? Here's a final set of basic rules to make a hollow corporation work:

- You must fix the design.
- There must be clear plans and specifications.
- Quality control procedures must be in place.
- Be willing to go overseas for production.
- You will need alternate sources of supply if let down by subcontractors.

I suggest that you test the hollow corporation format in whatever business you have in mind to start. In each case, you should experience some useful trade-offs. You may trade off price for quality control. If your business is fashion clothing, you must decide whether a "Made in U.S.A." label will be of greater benefit than importing lower-cost merchandise from Singapore. If you're into toys, the decision may be easier: Have the products made and packaged in China.

You will need to self-evaluate your personality as well as your ability to deal with people. No longer will you be the mad, introverted zealot cranking out the widgets in the garage. The hollow operation is going to favor the nimble negotiators—people who get on well with people. Perhaps you have the mechanical skills to build a new garage door opener, but do you have the smooth tongue to have others make and assemble it for you or to pressure them when they lag behind delivery schedule?

Beware of setting up a hollow corporation for a product that will cost more to buy than to make in-house. Part of the evaluation of a potential business is to determine this. But it is my belief that hollowing will be more cost effective (as well as more appropriate) than in-house manufacturing for most moonlighters.

Hollowing portends ominous prospects for the nation's work force. Yet if U.S. firms are shifting output to subcontractors, why then can't you do the same? It is the *moonlighter* who doesn't have the time or money or capacity to start up a factory. For the moonlighter, there is greater safety and more opportunity in *hollowing* a business than in struggling with all of the problems of running one.

# CHAPTER THIRTEEN

# *Real Estate*

Y ou can scratch the entrepreneur's itch in real estate without appearing to be in a business at all. And you can make more money—accidentally—than many people save throughout a lifetime of nine-to-five work. Your lucky break could be a piece of land purchased for investment, fixing up your home or a second home that is part of your retirement plan, or developing income producing properties.

It's entirely possible that your job skills can be brought into play. Your experience in purchasing can be useful in dealing with general contractors. An engineer already speaks the same language as the surveyor or architect. If you're in sales, the same closing techniques used in the daytime can be used to sell real estate by night. MBAs and CPAs can enjoy dealing with demographics, tax issues, and financing.

There are ample reasons making real estate suitable for the moonlighter. In a business sense, real estate figures favorably in the supply/demand equation: The supply is forever diminishing and the demand is steadily increasing. This explains why real estate values have become so breathtakingly inflated.

Real estate can also mean big bucks. You can make a fortune in widgets, but you gotta sell an awful lot of them. This is not the case with real estate. I know a couple who for years ran a fifteen-stool coffee shop. This entailed a lifetime of toil for them. Yet in earlier years they had acquired two R-4 lots in adjoining Glendale. In time they retired—not because of the thousands of gallons of coffee they had served—but on the profit from the sale of the property.

Real estate not only increases in value as a result of the supply/demand forces, but also as a function of the income you can extract from it. A shopping center is not valued by what it cost but by the capitalization of the rents. As a result, commercial properties shoot up in value as landlords receive higher and higher rents through cost-of-living adjustments.

Since the Tax Reform Act of 1986 (simplification, hah!) more of your time is required for tax planning. As the accounting firm, Arthur Andersen & Co., puts it, "Complexity is the hallmark of this legislation."

The real estate industry was a principal target, and the reforms specifically targeted tax-shelter abuses. You will require professional help, if only to prepare your tax return.

The major accounting firms publish booklets explaining the tax laws, and moonlighters in real estate should make use of them. One thing is clear: changes in IRS rules have never in the past taken the steam out of real estate. The inherent benefits are still there if we look for them.

The first step is to decide what specialty to engage in. Here are some convenient pigeonholes to look into:

▸ Residential: single family houses:
  Fix-up and trade-up your own residence.
  Fix-up spec houses.
  Build or buy spec houses or condos.
▸ Residential income units:
  Own and operate apartment buildings.
  Own a home-and-income apartment building.
▸ Commercial:
  Deal in shopping centers.
  Build-to-suit for credit tenants.
  Operate office buildings.
▸ Industrial:
  Develop industrial parks.
  Build-to-suit for credit tenants.
  Develop spec projects.
  Own and operate.
▸ Raw land:
  Invest in any of the above land uses.

Ownership of your own home offers the most important single opportunity to moonlight. Here are three suggestions to help you on your way.

First, *own* your home. Rest easy that your moonlight ambition to upgrade its value is not going to taint your home as a mere business enterprise. Quite the opposite will happen: Your improvement projects will create a common family goal of making it a better place to live.

Second, own a home on the largest piece of land you can afford. If land is too expensive, buy further away from the city where you will get more land for your dollar. The additional expense and time of commuting will be made up over the years by the appreciation of the property. It is the *land* that will appreciate most in value.

Third, do not compromise on quality of location. Live in a *better* neighborhood than you can afford, and take up the slack by being willing to buy, for a bargain, a fixer-upper than nobody else would be caught dead in. Your home will then give you ample opportunity to add sweat-equity value to it by work that you perform yourself.

Now, some houses are fixer-uppers and others are not. Homes are beyond redemption if the floor plan is seriously defective. Nobody wants to walk through the den to get from the kitchen to the dining room. But if a house is soundly built and planned, no matter how badly it has been maintained, it becomes an opportunity as a moonlight project.

The benefits of home ownership are greater than can be measured by cash equity. One doesn't need motivation to fix up a home; the driving force is called "pride of ownership." This supplies the energy needed to create a better place to live. Some people enjoy spending years moving from house to house, upgrading as they go and enjoying all of the following benefits:

- There are no conflict of interest problems.
- Most of us love doing it.
- It's a great hedge against inflation.
- Your whole family can participate.
- Your gains are tax deferred as you trade up.
- Your mortgage interest is deductible on both your first and second homes.

My wife and I recently acquired a new (fixer-upper) home. We immediately started the renovation activities, which took eight months to complete. No structural changes were made, but we did upgrade the ugly interior through extensive (professionally assisted) decorating changes. The outside, front and back, was completed renovated. I will confess that we both became obsessed with the project. After all, we were dedicating our energies to our new home.

Perhaps some of the time spent was unwarranted when compared with other pressing business matters (such as my job). What kept us so involved was this irresistible force, "pride of ownership." Judging the project purely as a moonlight activity, the results of our efforts have added well over $100,000 in equity to the home. Inflation has added another $100,000. But more important, we have a home we enjoy and are proud of.

A step away from this form of moonlighting is to buy and fix up houses, which are then sold at a profit, or to buy single family houses for rental income and appreciation. This is a popular option for moonlighters, especially when real estate is going through one of its periodic slumps.

Buying houses out of foreclosure is the game for some. While individual houses will spread your risk, the property management problems can be severe. It takes a high level of energy to withstand the constant crises of vacancies and torn-up carpeting. Be certain that the income from tenants will cover the expenses of mortgages, taxes, and upkeep. If this can be accomplished, over a long period of time two things should happen: the tenants will pay off the mortgage and the home will appreciate in value.

Another form of "house" moonlighting is to build houses for sale. "Spec" building is a decidedly risky activity and not for everyone. It's surely not something to be taken up on a grand scale. Yet it is exciting because while this can be called a single-product activity, you must be a jack-of-all-trades to pull it off. You will need skills in land acquisition, financing, architecture, construction, interior design, and selling.

This does not mean you should build *your* dream house. Instead you must carefully learn what the market demands and supply that demand in an exacting and not necessarily innovative way. You should use the best professionals when dealing with architecture and interior design. And find a very experienced real estate broker to acquire the land and ultimately to sell the house.

There are two basic rules in building spec homes. First, buy the most desirable available property, not the one lowest in price. This is not easy to practice, because we are programmed to buy the least expensive merchandise and not the top of the line. This rule we will call "Buy the Best," and it works when purchasing *any* type of real estate.

Once you've acquired the best property on the block, there will be a compelling temptation (believe me) to make the most of the location by building the biggest possible house. Don't do it. In fact, do just the opposite; the trick to successful spec building is to *underbuild*. Now the buyers will emerge, because you have the best location as well as an affordable home. The problem with overbuilding is that your price will be quite expensive for the neighborhood and more than likely out of the range of your desired market. And as you wait for a buyer, the interest expense eats away at your profit.

This lesson cost me thousands of dollars. I was once lucky enough to acquire the finest residential lot in town, which offered a spectacular view of the city. The site was so beautiful that I built a luxurious 5,000-square-foot spec home on it. It took a full year to sell, eventually at a break-even price. Had I built a 3,000-square-foot home, it would have been gobbled up by someone who could have afforded it and who could not have resisted the spectacular location.

Moonlighters are also well advised to deal in apartments. Residential income property does have some advantages. It serves the basic need for shelter. You can quickly adapt to inflation by increasing rents—except in those areas where there is rent control. Property management can either be handled by yourself or delegated to a professional manager. It is also a popular source of investment income for the retired moonlighter.

I know a recently retired airline pilot who has been moonlighting for twenty-five years by acquiring apartment buildings. He now owns a total of 100 units, located in buildings ranging from ten to twenty-five apartments. Over the years his average rental income has appreciated from $150 per month to $600 per month. Most of the maintenance and rental chores are now delegated to managers, leaving him free to travel. His moonlight business is the source of a substantial income that has made him financially independent.

A special niche for the apartment moonlighter is the home-and-income unit. The building will consist of three to ten apartments, including a deluxe owner's unit. Typically, the owner's unit is located in the front of the building and has special amenities such as fireplaces. These buildings are not usually large enough to create property management problems; maintenance and renting chores can be personally handled by the owner. Moonlighters in this field are normally very choosy in selecting tenants.

The home-and-income moonlighter can enjoy all of the amenities of home while having tenants pay for the expenses of maintaining it, including paying for the building. In Glendale, California, there are hundreds of old single-family houses built on what is now zoned as R-3 apartment property. Many of these houses have been torn down and replaced by home-and-income units.

Income real estate is definitely a cyclical business. In times of growth, the demand for space can exceed the supply. Developers will exude confidence; everybody and their moonlighting cousins will rapidly build new projects, continuing to do so until, inevitably, overcapacity is reached.

During times of excess capacity, the moonlighter may be confronted with empty buildings and falling rental rates; the income from tenants can be insufficient to make the mortgage payments and unless outside funds are available, owners go into default. Mortgage lenders begin repossessing the properties, wiping out the owners' equity. These properties are entered into the lenders' books as REO: "real estate owned." New construction abruptly comes to a standstill until the vacancies are absorbed, and the cycle starts up all over again.

During the foreclosure cycle, real estate moonlighters should approach lenders stuck with unwanted, embarrassing REO properties. Many lenders are willing to turn properties over—without profit or down payment—simply to get them off the books. They just hate having these numbers appear on their financial statements!

Before approaching the lender, you must locate new sources of income sufficient to service the pre-existing debt. Have enough cash to carry the building through the negative phase of the cash-flow cycle. Later, in better times with higher occupancy and rents, the properties can gain enormously in value.

It's J. Paul Getty's old technique: Buy when all others are selling. The drop in oil prices brought great hardships to Texas and the Rocky

Mountain states. This is when fortunes are lost (by those who built at the top of the cycle) and *made* by those who take advantage of calamity by buying at the bottom. Will oil prices rise again? Will overbuilding eventually be absorbed? In both cases, history tells us yes, to the eventual glee of the (hopefully moonlight) opportunists.

You must surely have a personal story about what you *might* have made in some piece of real estate, yet didn't because the deal was passed up. Let me tell you mine. I was building apartments in Los Angeles when construction accelerated to a frenzy. At the time there was an expanding demand for housing. Like all real estate cycles, it topped out quickly and vacancies soared. Developers woke up to find themselves with mortgage obligations they couldn't meet, and hundreds of apartment projects went into foreclosure.

I suddenly found that the demand (not to mention financing) for new income units had vanished. Instead, there were thousands of vacant apartments. Had I possessed shrewd foresight, I would have ended up on *easy* street. I missed the opportunity of a lifetime to acquire apartment buildings with no investment. The opportunity was right under my nose and in my own field of expertise.

To make matters worse (not having apartment construction to keep me occupied) I proceeded into a business that I knew nothing about: the franchising of restaurants. This venture ultimately failed. Had I remained in the apartment business by beginning to buy them up, I would have saved myself and my family a great deal of misery. You get the point: stick to your specialty through thick and thin, looking for opportunities in bad times as well as in good times.

Commercial development is shunned by many moonlighters because it's unfamiliar territory. Yet this is the reason it is perhaps one of the better opportunities. Commercial real estate is rightly considered a more sophisticated field than residential real estate. In the past, commercial developers usually started out as residential carpenters who eventually graduated into commercial or industrial projects.

Commercial development is the choice for MBAs who spent their internships in commercial brokerage firms or as apprentices with large developers. The marketing, financial, and tax aspects have become so complex that commercial development now attracts CPAs instead of carpenters.

All types of income-producing real estate (residential, commercial, or industrial) can produce spectacular earnings. The professional developers are keenly aware of these potential profit margins, but investors who buy them are not. The reason for this opportunity should be understood by the real estate moonlighter. It boils down to a matter of apples and oranges.

When you sell an apple, the price you can get is based on the cost of the apple plus the markup. Selling income-producing real estate is different. The costs are apples, but the selling price is oranges. Costs are made up of land, buildings and site work (apples), but the selling price is determined by a multiplication of the income (oranges). The margin of profit between these indirectly related factors *can* be enormous.

This explains why developers are driven to extract higher rents from tenants. I can illustrate this by a single example. Let's assume that you, the moonlighter, build a small convenience shopping center. Your sale price will be based on capitalizing your total rents. Let's assume the going capitalization rate is 10 percent (that is, the center can sell for a 10 percent return). For every additional one hundred dollars per month of rent you can negotiate, the value of the project is increased by $12,000: ($100 × 12 months, divided by ten percent).

Shopping centers can be pursued in a number of ways. You can develop projects in order to keep them for income and investment, or to sell them for profit. You can also purchase an existing center and rehabilitate it to enhance the income.

A note of caution follows. Many old service stations currently being purchased for mini-centers have leaky underground tanks. New environmental laws can result in the necessity for decontamination costing hundreds of thousands of dollars. Don't close escrow until the seller has satisfied all state and federal environmental agencies that the tanks have been removed and the soil is not contaminated. Otherwise you may become responsible for any clean-up costs. And never agree to hold the seller not liable for rectifying these problems.

The best opportunities for the moonlighter in commercial real estate are to secure leases with long-term *credit* tenants. This can be done on a build-to-suit basis or by having credit tenants occupy space you've already developed. There are a number of advantages:

- ▸ You can finance the building on the strength of the lease itself.
- ▸ You will not lose sleep over unpaid or slow-paid rents.
- ▸ You won't have to worry about upkeep or increases in taxes (the tenant will pay them).
- ▸ The value of the property will continue to rise based on your cost-of-living rent adjustments.

For the moment I have some reservations about developing small centers. Retailers say that there are only three periods in the life of a product: pre-peak, peak, and post-peak. Small-center developments are presently edging into the post-peak period. There is a tell-tale symptom for this, namely that everybody is in on it.

UCLA holds a one-day seminar each year on "The Shopping Center Game." The sessions are worth UCLA's efforts, because a lot of people are interested in playing the game. Fifteen hundred would-be developers pay $95 each to attend them; hundreds are turned away each year because the grand ballroom of the Marriott Hotel can't handle the overflow.

It's why Joe Kennedy got out of the stock market just before the crash of 1929. One day when he stopped for a shoe shine on Wall Street, the shoeshine man was reading the *Wall Street Journal* and offering tips: "Buy oils and rails. They're gonna hit the sky." That night Kennedy told his wife, Rose, that a market everyone could play (and a shoeshine boy could predict) was no market for him.

Industrial real estate is another field usually left to specialists. This is not to say that the specialists are always full-time professionals. A southern California moonlighting orthodontist became so successful in developing industrial parks for small tenants that he left his practice to engage in it full time.

We have a city here in California (appropriately named Industry) where for thirty years Commerce Construction Company has been building concrete tilt-up buildings ranging from 40,000 square feet to 250,000. Most are built on speculation. One of their new 200,000-square-foot buildings was recently leased to General Electric for use as a distribution center. Commerce Construction can take G.E.'s lease to an insurance company and borrow money on this assured source of debt repayment. If a moonlighter owns industrial property in a favorable location, credit-worthy firms will frequently be attracted to such built-to-suit (leased) facilities, so their cash is not tied up in land and buildings.

Real estate can be leveraged like no other business activity. But real estate debt must be serviced by rents. Spec home builders gravitate to apartment buildings or commercial projects because there are tenants to make those payments when the project is completed. The spec house or condo, unsold, becomes a hemorrhage of negative cash flow. The agony of defeat in this business can often be linked to a poor location or optimistic overborrowing.

Yet most downtrends in real estate have been cushioned by long-term inflation. And when every project is selling out or renting up, it's easy to miss (or wilfully ignore) the telltale signs that the cycle is topping out. When a real estate recession occurs during a period of deflation, the highly leveraged operators are ruthlessly cleaned out.

John Connally returned to private life in Texas to make it big in real estate. When he started, he was worth six million dollars. He felt confident there would be no end to the twin booms in oil and real estate. He never incorporated, and together with a partner borrowed about $60 million to finance shopping centers, luxury condominiums, and office buildings. Admittedly, even pessimists did not foresee that oil would drop from $32 a barrel to $9. But when it did, the boom ended for oil, for real estate and, sadly, for Connally as well.

I recommend that all real estate moonlighters should get a real estate license. The real estate schools specialize in preparation for the licensing examination. They are well worth the price of admission whether you go for the license or not. They will furnish a treasure chest of knowledge concerning fundamental real estate law and terminology.

Limited partnerships have traditionally been popular for passive investors in real estate. For you, the moonlighter, these syndications do not offer freedom to be in charge (a prime objective for the moonlighter) nor sufficient opportunity for quick profit. The general partners will be taking the cream off the projects in the form of fees. It's better to do it all yourself.

Real estate attracts bright, persuasive people. The dollar rewards are large—the desire for them so great—that the traditional firm handshake should not be relied upon. I'm sad to say you'll find that ethical conduct can and will stop at the buck. Every aspect of your real estate dealings should be legally documented, accurately and completely. By having every agreement in writing, you will be protected from some shocking disappointments.

I think it's better to subcontract work to general contractors than to take on the work yourself. The competition among general contractors will generally result in their building efficiently and at the right (fixed) price. Experienced general contractors know who the good and reasonably priced subcontractors are—but you generally won't. The subs look to them for regular future work—and not to you.

And with the services of a general contractor, your time becomes free to concentrate on other aspects of development rather than being tied up with construction details. Most experienced commercial developers use general contractors rather than operating as contractors.

But in some cases the moonlighter can act as an "owner-builder" rather than using a general contractor. It will depend on your experience and desire as to whether it is feasible to get involved in subcontracting and supervision of trades. The first time around can be traumatic; key subcontractors can be helpful in guiding you around the traps. A risk of conflict of interest with your job could exist when going owner-builder, unless other members of the family are willing and able to take over the daytime responsibilities.

Real estate is clearly a field in which specialists do better than the casual players, but any specialty can be pursued by simply imitating what successful specialists in the field are doing. One way to learn is to join appropriate trade associations. If you're interested in apartments, join the Apartment Association; if you have trouble with a tenant, their legal department can advise you. If you're into shopping centers, join the I.C.S.C. (International Council of Shopping Centers). The more you are involved in these activities, the fewer mistakes you will make. And mistakes in real estate can be dear ones.

Many moonlighters attend real estate seminars. They all make the same promise: how to acquire real estate with no money down. "How I made a million dollars" seminars may divulge some tricks in dealing with sellers and disclose some innovative (if dubious) methods of financing. Yet I am skeptical about get-rich-quick schemes. It may be *possible* to finance out 100 percent, but the debt service can become difficult to maintain.

As a moonlight developer, you'll be dealing with planning departments that have discretionary authority in the approval of projects. No longer can you rely on zoning codes to determine what the rules will be. You will be faced with planning review boards that can often be unreasonable in their decisions. Many cities have redevelopment agencies authorized to impose conditions even more stringent than those established by local codes.

The way to handle planning authorities is, first of all, to communicate with them on the personal level. Then just ride the horse in the direction the horse is going. There is nothing to be gained in fighting City Hall. A shopping center developer in Palm Springs was so frustrated with the unreasonable demands of city agencies that he finally threw up his hands and sold off his rights to the property.

The purchaser of this property was from, of all places, Melbourne, Australia. He knew nothing of the demands that had been made by the authorities. But the center eventually turned out to be enormously successful. I later asked the Australian what his secret was, and he said simply, "I went into City Hall and told them that I would do anything they wanted me to do—and did it."

Now, obviously there will be times when unreasonable conditions will make a project infeasible. In such cases you should unemotionally drop the project and seek out the next one. But never go into an escrow without the contingency that approvals must first be obtained from the necessary authorities for whatever you have in mind.

How does the moonlighter find locations? By driving the streets. You will not know the true worth of a property until you have an intimate knowledge of comparative values. Six years ago my wife and I purchased a home in Palm Springs. For six months we looked at all of the homes for sale in the neighborhood we were interested in. With this study under our belts, we *knew* when the right property, at the right price, with the right financing, finally came our way. We pounced on it so fast that the seller wanted to consider another, higher bid the day after our purchase price was accepted. The only thing that kept the deal together was that it was in writing.

I know an eminently successful commercial real estate broker who determined his moonlighting goal years ago: to go into debt for five million

94

dollars. His plan was simple. He made sure that the properties selected were good enough to be rented by sound tenants. In each case he had twenty-five-year financing, and he looked upon his projects as property that twenty-five years down the road would be his. By then the tenants will have paid for all of them. Over the years inflation resulted in higher and higher rents, and the properties eventually were worth far more than he ever dreamed.

To sum up, real estate is especially good territory for the moonlighter. You will need a feel for big bucks and a sense of prudent optimism. If you start with the right location, buyers or tenants will beat a path to your door. And a good location can cushion some of the other mistakes we make.

Real estate is definitely an emotionally satisfying activity. Aside from the material rewards, you gain a great deal of personal satisfaction when you start with dirt and end up with a completed home or shopping center. You have made something out of nothing.

Best of all, dealing in real estate is generally not perceived as a form of clandestine business activity likely to conflict with your regular line of work. Your employer will probably be more inclined to admire your real estate moonlighting than to see it as a threat to your job loyalty. More than likely it will be viewed by your boss as a means by which some, quite acceptably, get rich.

# CHAPTER FOURTEEN

# Our Daily Bread

Jimmie Durante used to say, "*Everybody* wants to get inta da act!" Moonlighters are flocking to the kitchen because everybody can find opportunity in food—from the cheesecake baker to the would-be tycoon. Even as a sideline business, food offers a great diversity of choices requiring relatively small investments and a minimum of risk.

As long as you can lift that rolling pin, you have a source of making money outside of your regular job. Recipes that begin at home on the stove can find their way into supermarkets everywhere. Margaret Rudkin baked preservative-free whole wheat bread for her children in her kitchen to get through hard times. She started Pepperidge Farm in 1937. The firm so far has reached $455 million in sales.

If you have a technical or professional background, you may be disdainful about putting on an apron. At the outset I confess that I was. I was looking for a real, hard core *business*—one that dealt with manufacturing products, not cooking them. Don't make the mistake of disparaging a food opportunity. I now regret not following my Aunt Myrtle's suggestion to open a pie shop. She was a fabulous baker, and her pies (you'll have to take my word for it) surpassed any that have been made before or since.

In the food industry, the little guy can take on the big guy and win. This "David and Goliath" aspect is not always found in other fields. David's advantage here is that he is better motivated and informed than Goliath. Eating is a very personal matter, and this is something to which big-buck interests in big organizations are not always sensitive. Your competitor in the restaurant across the street may have spent three million dollars in decor, yet you can triumph as David did.

You can do this by creating a dining experience within your own humble limitations that will leave your guests eager to tell their friends. You can start without the benefit of an established reputation and most likely without advertising. But within a week you will experience the restaurateurs' upward spiral; your guests not only come back, they tell their friends who come back and tell *their* friends . . . and so on.

The public is always game for a new food experience. There will always be enthusiasts out there just waiting to give you a try. But if you mistreat that first wave of customers, they will form a relentless army of detractors who will not only fail to return but will pass their judgment on to others. You will be zapped by word of mouth before you even know what hit you.

All categories of food businesses offer the following advantages:

- ► Food is an ongoing, undiminishing market (people must eat).
- ► You have the option of exploiting a worldwide demand or satisfying a single local appetite.
- ► Food is appropriate for exploiting a single product.
- ► It's a business that can (and should be) started with a minimum amount of investment.
- ► It furnishes an opportunity to exploit your sophisticated marketing and management skills.
- ► You can eliminate competition by attaining a unique level of quality.
- ► If you love to cook (it may be a single recipe) you can make a business out of what you're good at in the kitchen.

Nobody's going to unseat Sara Lee, Planter's Peanuts, or Frito-Lay. All have risen above their competition by a simple doctrine called Quality Without Compromise®. As you can see, this is a registered trademark (for See's Candies), but the slogan says everything about what it takes to win in the food business.

While the restaurant business is a favorite, it is not the only food endeavor open to moonlighters. There are other opportunities for the moonlighter that are even more appropriate. And in food-related businesses, anyone can get into the act. Regardless of your age, your ethnic background, or your level of education and sophistication, moonlighting can be pursued in:

- ► Restaurants
- ► Marketing packaged food products
- ► Cottage food industries
- ► Selling through mail order
- ► Catering
- ► Cooking schools
- ► Cook books and journalism

The restaurant business in the United States is a $160 billion industry, and there's always room for newcomers. It's a hands-on business demanding long hours; but for moonlighters who have the support of family members or partners, it can be overwhelmingly enticing.

Restaurants are divided into three categories: fast food, family restaurants, and dinner houses. Fast food can provide an opportunity for the mom-and-pop operation or become the start of a chain. A family restaurant can go either way: as a multiple-unit coffee-shop type or as an individual restaurant run by a family (a strong possibility for some moonlighters). Dinner houses require highly trained professionals and specialized formats, usually ethnic in character.

It is possible to spend a fortune to open a restaurant. Many start-up restaurateurs are willing to throw big bucks at a new venture. But significantly—and unfortunately—most are not prepared to throw *themselves* into the business. Delegation may be the acceptable business school way of management, but this rule does not apply to starting a restaurant.

I don't think a restaurant can be successfully run by an absentee moonlighter. There may be some businesses where you can take a passive role, but not here. It's not only labor intensive, but requires that every aspect of preparation and service be maintained without compromise on an unremitting basis. These are not easily delegated to a manager. Therefore, some kind of partner will be required to assume responsibility for the day-to-day operation.

The best way to learn the restaurant business is to work for someone else first. If you're interested in a delicatessen, pick out the most successful one in town and work for it. There are no other schools for learning the business. Those of us who skipped this step (usually because of misguided confidence) have paid dearly in the form of making avoidable mistakes. I also recommend you begin by doing *everything* yourself and later on, when you do begin to delegate, no one can fool you about how to run the business.

Successful restaurants offer high value to their patrons. Rather than slicing the ham thinner, emphasis is put on providing more satisfying portions. An operation can run profitably at a high food cost despite food representing one of the two major costs, the other being labor. The *sum* of these two expenses is the critical figure on the profit-and-loss statement.

A restaurant can absorb a higher food cost if the added value attracts more customers, because the resulting high volume of sales will reduce the percentage cost of labor. For example, it may be smarter to operate at 40 percent food cost and 20 percent labor for a total of 60 percent than to operate at 30 percent food and 30 percent labor. In the first instance, the customer is getting a whole third more in value (40 percent vs. 30 percent of the dollar will end up between the lips).

Restaurants can be profitable from opening day, so they are frequently referred to as "cash cows." Most other businesses devour cash in the form of working capital, inventory, and receivables. However, an all-cash business has its drawbacks—in this particular case, skimming. You may at first assume this to be a juicy although illicit perk (the grubby merchant slyly raiding the till). The more likely possibility is that your employees will be stealing from *you*. It's better to learn about cash control before you start than figure it out later in order to plug a cash hemorrhage.

For the ambitious moonlighter, fast food offers the best opportunity to expand a single successful pilot unit into a chain. But to create a successful chain takes a gifted entrepreneur because of the requisite skills. You must initially be willing to put on that apron and, hands-on, create a successful pilot operation. Transforming your prototype into a chain will call for altogether different abilities in real estate development, management, and finance. Many who succeed with a single outlet have come to grief when taking on the expansion into multiple units.

For moonlighters with a chain in mind, it's important to thoroughly prove the viability of the prototype unit before even thinking of the second location. Solving problems as they crop up in a single unit is difficult enough; to have them surface in two or three simultaneously can soon become unmanageable.

The fast-food business can take much credit for a basic shift, still taking place, in American eating habits. We have more money to spend but less time to spend it, so we are eating more of our meals in restaurants — and this shift holds good for breakfast, lunch, and dinner. Fast-food restaurateurs have tested every imaginable concept, but every successful operation shares certain basic traits:

- ▸ Speed of service
- ▸ High value and low cost
- ▸ Quality
- ▸ Cleanliness
- ▸ Consistency
- ▸ Elimination of tipping

When Ray Kroc first saw the McDonald brothers' operation, his strongest impression was that working people were being served immediately. The fast-food business became a time and motion study aimed at offering speed of service, both at the counter and at the drive-up window.

Quality is another factor in the success of fast food. There is a widespread belief that fast food is junk food. But compromise is not tolerated in the quality of the ingredients themselves (unhealthy as they may be). Heaven help the fast-food operator who begins to cut corners in the quality of the shortening or the cheese. On the contrary, quality is an absolutely vital ingredient in the rapid growth of the industry. The fast-food chains have developed standards that the moonlighter must not only emulate but match if the venture is to survive.

Fast food also liberated the American restaurant customer from tipping, thereby making meals all the more affordable in comparison to eating at home. This and the previously mentioned factors have collectively changed the eating habits and dietary preferences of the American public.

There's a lot to be said for sticking to specialty items that have widespread appeal and are basic to our diet. The three most important of these are, of course, hamburgers, hamburgers, and hamburgers. You can verify from your own experience that most successful operations are filling a widespread, if specialized, demand rather than providing less popular products. (We eat more hamburgers than we do hot dogs.)

The eclectic menu does not do well in fast food—for example, selling hamburgers, pizza, hot dogs, and tacos. The identity of the operation becomes blurred in the mind of the customer. When decision time comes, the customer will opt for the restaurant specializing in the desired food. If you want hamburgers, the choice will be McDonald's or Burger King; if ice cream, you'll go to Baskin Robbins or Häagen-Dazs—but not a convenience store, even if that's nearest. Customers have a great number of specialists to choose from.

The basic rules to follow in fast food can all be learned from Ray Kroc. He once said, "If I had a brick for every time I've repeated the phrase Q.S.C. and V. (Quality, Service, Cleanliness and Value), I think I'd probably be able to bridge the Atlantic Ocean with them." From its first day of operation, McDonald's has never deviated from these fundamentals. Q.S.C. and V. became the watchword: a high-quality product just about everybody loves, instantly served in immaculately clean stores at prices anyone can afford.

Family restaurants form the dividing line between fast food and dinner houses. They include coffee shops, specialty restaurants such as pizza houses, and an increasing array of ethnic restaurants. And as with fast food, a chain requires altogether different management skills than are required in operating a single unit.

Operating a dinner house is only for the highly trained and thoroughly experienced professional. This is not an appropriate business for the moonlighter, unless you have an unusually good background as a restaurateur. You might consider it if running a dinner house would become an extension of fine cooking skills that have been routinely practiced in your home, perhaps for generations.

Many well-heeled entrepreneurs who have succeeded in other fields are drawn into the dinner house business. You may indeed be a gourmet, but it's a mistake to assume that dining in fine restaurants is even a beginning qualification for operating one. The key attraction is probably the quasi-celebrity aspect you'll enjoy by owning this kind of a business. How delightful is the prospect of stroking the patrons with chit-chat about the fettuccine! But the inexperienced ex-tycoon is typically forever preoccupied with making hasty apologies, one eye meanwhile glued on the cash register—and the other on the back door.

While restaurants attract entrepreneurs like bees to honey, there are other food businesses offering more appropriate opportunities for the moonlighter. First, there is the marketing of packaged food products. The markup in food between harvest and shelf is astounding. A box of corn flakes costs $2.50—which is roughly the price of a bushel of corn! The reason is the long pipeline that food must traverse between field and plate. The expense of transportation and packaging now exceeds the cost of food products themselves. Yet it is in this markup structure that opportunity emerges for a part-time business.

The marketing of packaged food is locked into a distribution network of brokers, wholesalers, and supermarkets and is dominated by the leading brands. Once a brand is established, it becomes a source of steady profits. Kellogg controls 42 percent of the $5.5 billion dry cereal business, bringing the company a 46 percent return on equity.

Americans in the past have shunned generic labels for brand names such as Heinz catsup and Campbell's soup. The result is that operating margins on big-name products can run as much as twice that of generic names. Smaller food concerns have had a difficult time holding their own against the big brands.

Yet nothing is fixed in business. "Wholesale" outlets are now playing an expanding role. The Price Club and its many new competitors are beginning to pull in the big bucks of consumer food purchases.

Your local supermarket is beginning to display more generic labels side by side with the highly advertised brands, and at far lower prices. Container costs are being slashed by packaging products into larger bags, boxes, or cans, which may be less attractive to the eye but have enormous impact on the price per ounce of product. I recently took a survey of some food prices, first at a wholesale outlet (The Price Club), and then at a large chain supermarket (Alpha Beta). The astonishing result, based on price per pound of product, was that supermarket prices were on the average 44 percent higher than those of the wholesaler.

| | Wholesaler | | Supermarket | | |
|---|---|---|---|---|---|
| Item | lb./Container | Price/lb. | lb./Container | Price/lb. | Percentage Higher |
| Canned peaches | 6.75 | $ .38 | 1.81 | $ .52 | 37 |
| Brand X mayo | 3 | .86 | 3 | .94 | 9 |
| Granul. sugar | 25 | .31 | 10 | .36 | 16 |
| Brand Y flour | 25 | .12 | 25 | .21 | 75 |
| Raisins | 4 | .75 | 1.5 | 1.12 | 49 |
| Brand Z jam | 2.62 | 1.05 | 1.12 | 1.95 | 86 |
| Brand A coffee | 3 | 3.05 | 3 | 3.30 | 8 |
| Apples | 11 | .45 | 1 | .69 | 53 |
| Oranges | 13 | .41 | 1 | .59 | 44 |
| Froz. roughy | 3 | 4.50 | 1 | 5.99 | 33 |
| Potato chips | 1 | 1.89 | 1 | 1.89 | 0 |
| Tortilla chips | 5 | .67 | 1 | 1.49 | 120 |

It is significant that the widest differences are in generic products. Name brands such as Brand X Mayonnaise and Brand A coffee have such closely controlled price structures that the wholesaler's price is not significantly reduced from that charged in the supermarket. This suggests all the more opportunity for generic products to vanquish well-known brand names in the wholesale environment.

We have been accustomed to limiting our grocery shopping at discount stores to household staples such as paper goods, cleaning supplies, and other bulk items, but not any more; the public is now buying even regular food staples by the half-case rather than by the can, because the price per unit is so much cheaper.

Smart and Final Company of California operates ninety-five discount cash-and-carry stores, whose customers for many years were mainly restaurants and commercial institutions. They have now become a hybrid animal, selling as much to the public as to businesses.

Moonlighters with uniquely good food products can benefit from this groundswell of "wholesale" public buying. You will pay essentially the same ingredient cost as Frito-Lay but not be burdened with their built-in expenses.

You can undersell established producers who are locked into a maze of expensive packaging, overhead, advertising, distribution, and markups. If a wholesale outlet can be convinced of your product quality and reliability, you can expand into a large operation.

I speak on this with some experience. Since 1986, Yum Yum Donuts has engaged in the sale of prepackaged doughnuts through the Price Club. The participating Yum Yum shops making the products have added this volume to their over-the-counter sales. The added complications of going into this aspect of food marketing are well worth your efforts.

Successful food purveyors consistently stress their dedication to quality. Nothing we buy is subject to greater critical judgement than the food we eat. You can produce cheap TV sets or shoes, and customers will buy them; unappetizing foods appeal to no one, not even the value conscious. In the food business, as in others, volume can be expanded by reducing prices. But if a food price is reduced at the expense of quality, the seller is in for some unhappy surprises.

If you have an uncommonly good recipe for a single item, you have the key to success in food. Dave Snyder knew how to make a buttermilk bar so good that hungry people would steal for it. He began producing them by hand in an open frying kettle and sold them to a few local catering trucks. As his business grew, he gradually began shifting production to automatic equipment.

It was a classic bootstrap process: the higher the sales, the more Dave could afford new machinery. The more automation, the lower was his pricing, propelling sales even higher. That single product is now made entirely by automation; Dave's Buttermilk Bars has grown into a large business. New competition would have great difficulty in matching this combination of quality and low cost.

A common fear of those starting a business is that products selling today may become obsolete tomorrow. A business can either succeed or falter because of the changing demands of style, fads, or technology. Somebody will come out with a better mousetrap; but food itself does not change. Dave Snyder started his business back in 1960. His product is now produced differently, but otherwise is essentially the same.

Dave enjoyed security over the years because eating habits are very slow to change. But when they do, you had better be prepared to shift with them. Consumer preference is now shifting toward baked goods (muffins, for example). If you're in the business of making doughnuts, you'd better think about installing an oven alongside the fryer.

Cookies serve as an example of how a single product can be built into a large business. Wally Amos wasn't in the food business at all, but worked for the William Morris talent agency. As a moonlighter he made a high-quality chocolate chip cookie and successfully combined this with his background in promotion. The result was the "Famous Amos" chain of retail cookie shops that has spawned so many imitators. Wally was also successful in getting into the packaged food business as an outgrowth of his retail chain.

If you have a single, really good recipe and any flair for business, then your specialty can spell opportunity. For those who wish to moonlight in a small way, there are many possibilities for successful cottage businesses. One example is to make desserts for fine restaurants. Perhaps you have an old family recipe for fruitcake. You may know how to make peanut brittle so unusually appetizing that it could not be duplicated in a commercial kitchen at any price.

Another cottage food business worth examining is catering for receptions and parties. This business is focusing more and more on catering meals that are served in homes, and not always for special occasions. Women in jobs don't have the time to prepare fancy dinners. At-home entertaining can be revived by the services of moonlight caterers. My wife and I recently gave a small party, and most of the menu was catered by a physician's wife. She specializes in French cuisine and does this work as a joyful expression of her entrepreneurial inclinations.

Food catering can be expanded into a large and sophisticated operation. Food catering trucks that serve industrial plants are no longer "garbage wagons" but mobile high-tech kitchens that prepare hot foods to order at prices lower than fast-food restaurants. Catering to special customers such as airlines or institutions can also be a profitable moonlight venture.

Mail order is yet another segment of the food business to consider. If your product can be packaged and shipped, it can probably be sold by mail. I just received a box of Texas grapefruit as a Christmas gift—a delightful surprise. This is the kind of specialized line that could be easily done as a sideline business. (Direct-mail opportunities for moonlighters are covered in Chapter 15.)

Harry and David's Fruit-of-the-Month Club has gone this route and expanded to a nationwide operation. Their orchard-fresh delicacies are too good (expensive) to be found in the market, and these unique gifts can be delivered on three-month or twelve-month plans. They ship highly perishable products that you would be amazed to receive on your doorstep: even pears and grapes! Once again, their secret ingredient is Quality without Compromise®. The coupling of mail order and food offers intriguing possibilities for the moonlighter, because both are so appropriate for a sideline operation.

For those with a flair for teaching, after-hours cooking schools find a limited but affluent market. (French nouvelle cuisine is a current favorite.) If you're into wine, there may be wine-tasting classes or wine country excursions to consider.

Food hobbyists as well as professionals have found satisfaction in publishing cookbooks. A woman whose experience was gained entirely in her own kitchen recently published a book devoted to chocolate recipes that became a great success. However, writing cookbooks should not be undertaken as a surefire way of making money. Cookbooks written in the moonlight can provide author satisfaction, but don't count on any profit. (Although the late Victor Chapin, a friend of mine who was a literary agent, paid his rent for years through Craig Claiborne's *The New York Times Cook Book*.)

Finally, be aware that the preparation of food is closely regulated by health laws, and in some cases compliance is verified by federal inspectors. Before making a commitment on a place of business, consult with the local health department to find out what will be required in terms of cleaning and possible remodeling.

In selecting a food product, I would suggest that you consider foods perceived to be healthful. Yogurt shops are enjoying a spectacular growth rate, but ice cream stores are not. Sales of fish and poultry are on the rise, but the egg business is in sad decline. I am not suggesting you run out and open up a yogurt store, but emphasis on the healthfulness of a food product is going to enhance your success.

It is possible to go *too* far in emphasizing the health benefits of food. The problem is that the appeal can become too limited. The ideal is to have the best of both worlds: sell what people want to eat, but slant the marketing as much as possible to the fact that the product is also good for you.

Some examples of products with widespread appeal but which are also perceived to be good for you are mesquite-broiled fish, natural grain breads, low-fat dairy products, baked goods, and pasta. (Also note that McDonald's milk is low fat.)

A health-oriented copycat of Wendy's, "D'Lights," recently filed Chapter 11. It was a shame; the concept was sound, and the initial operation was a bang-up success. The idea was to sell a hamburger with low-fat meat, low-calorie cheese, and a whole wheat bun — the best of both worlds! The concept was fine, but the management went out of control. Imprudent spending and rushed growth left franchisees in less-than-optimum locations. Good ideas must be backed up by good management.

Every day you're in the food business, there will be a sword hanging over your head: each item you sell must be as good as the last one. A Los Angeles restaurant was packed for thirty years and when the owner suddenly died, the operation was taken over by an inexperienced operator. It closed within six months. The customers verdict came down with the speed and finality of Roman justice: thumbs down.

Not everybody can get into a business of their choice because the constraints of time or money will get in the way. It's not that way with food. If you emerge with a product that the world really wants, the masses are going to beat a path to your door. Here's your final reminder of the moonlighter's guide for success in the food business:

- ▸ Offer quality without compromise.
- ▸ Give high value.
- ▸ Stay with healthy foods.
- ▸ Specialize.

# CHAPTER FIFTEEN

# Direct Marketing

L et's admit it: Operating a moonlight business *is* a juggling act. But what if you could run the operation without any face-to-face contacts at all? Direct marketing can take much of the juggling out of the act. The need for a traditional retail store is circumvented, along with the accompanying demands on time and pocketbook. Instead, advertising is used to sell products.

In this chapter, I will first describe what kind of businesses make up direct marketing and then outline the advantages and disadvantages. Finally, you'll get some specific tips on how to go about starting this kind of a moonlight business.

The two major forces in merchandising, direct marketing and retail outlets, stand in stark opposition to each other. Direct marketing eliminates the customary expenses of retailing while at the same time incurring horrific advertising expenses. On the other hand, high-volume stores can minimize the customary retailing expenses by operating out of bare-bones outlets with the narrowest of profit margins—while incurring no advertising costs whatever.

*Business Week*, in a cover story, titled "Home Shopping," reported a study by Retail Planning Associates demonstrating that consumers who had just eaten a meal were 25 percent more likely to buy clothing than hungry shoppers. Jeff St. Clair, research director at RPA, explained, "The guy's sitting back with a beer in hand, he's relaxed, his guard is down." This "full stomach" theory helps explain the success rate of direct marketing (where the customer buys after supper) as well as the recent boom in the catalog industry, which has grown 59 percent between 1981 and 1986, reaching sales of $50 billion a year.

Direct marketing got its start in mail order; this is still the backbone of the business. The most recent growth in direct marketing has been on television, first through 800 numbers on commercial stations and more recently through home shopping on cable TV stations. In addition to television, a wide range of other advertising media is employed: radio, daily newspapers, Sunday newspapers, telephone sales, direct selling, and even comic books and foreign media.

In its present infancy, TV home shopping is a step forward for the shop-at-home industry. Retailing by television now includes boutique UHF channels selling only one narrow line of products. Home shoppers are snapping up everything from mink coats to airline travel tours. TV home shopping can be a schlocky blend of game show antics and old-fashioned hucksterism, but it's turning into big business. And to help matters, most people capable of signing their name have credit cards.

Can home-shopping programs get people to sit down and shop seriously? The TV product image must be so strong that viewers will decide then and there to reach for the phone. Some believe that its current success will decrease greatly once the initial novelty has worn off. In contrast, mail-order catalog shoppers can browse through pages rather than sitting impatiently through tooting horns and tacky jewelry.

Mail order has something for everybody. For example, some firms are presently testing the sale and rental of videotapes by mail. This would fill the gap between VCR owners and self-help videotape producers. Even the large retail video stores haven't yet stocked self-help tapes, so direct mail catalogs may have a profitable product line to exploit.

A recent entry into the field is "The Video Schoolhouse." Their catalog includes 3,500 titles of how-to and informational videotapes on diverse topics such as piloting an airplane, dog training, learning to play golf "the Jack Nicklaus way," speed reading, foreign languages, home and car repair, and, of course, workout tapes. Whether video mail order will be successful in absorbing the enormous expense of advertising remains to be seen. It is clearly not a field for the start-up moonlighter to experiment in. But if other pioneers prove it to be successful, then a copycat opportunity may open up.

While television is the medium highest in impact, radio carries more direct-marketing advertising because it is more affordable for the small business. Some radio advertisers will build their entire programming around the product they sell. In Los Angeles there is a daily talk show on real estate sponsored and conducted by a syndicator of shopping centers. The program topics focus on real estate investment. The sponsor plucks limited partners for the shopping center syndications from the show's receptive audience.

Even good old-fashioned direct selling (pitched by professionals or not-so-professionals at Tupperware parties) is still alive and well. This business has survived being flogged by recent cooling-off laws giving buyers the right to cancel orders once they have returned to their senses.

Still, Amway and Mary Kay have become favorite moonlight activities for tens of thousands of moonlighting quasi-entrepreneurs. A. L. Williams has more than 100,000 representatives selling life insurance on a direct basis. Their business card (in the fine print) discloses that the firm is "a co-op of independent businessmen and women marketing life insurance and other financial products."

In some lines of direct selling, leads can be provided by public records (such as those involving births, deaths, and marriages). The cost of advertising is replaced by the expense of commissions paid to direct salespersons (usually independent agents) who follow up these leads. Firms selling photographic services and equipment use this method, selling primarily to new parents in small towns.

Direct marketing is not so much a matter of selling certain items; it is one of selling lines of items. An individual item cannot normally support a business, but a proven item can become one of a line of items that over time makes up a successful direct-marketing program. The flat-tire inflator (canned air) is a successful item still sold in many mail-order catalogs; but although it is a proven success, it could not be relied upon as a single product to sustain a business in itself; it must be incorporated in a line of items sold as auto accessories.

For the moonlighter, there are ample reasons to consider the direct-marketing route. The very thought of selling directly to customers sitting in their living rooms tickles the imagination. Even better is the prospect of deploying computer-managed information banks, satellite TV, and plastic credit. You can select from an ever-expanding array of formats including:

- mail order
- catalog selling
- TV marketing
- telemarketing (telephone selling)
- cable home shopping
- direct selling (an exception to the no "face-to-face contact" rule)

Each of these in turn has its own subspecialties depending on what you're selling and the advertising media you use. For example, the sale of gourmet foods, books, and shoes are all established mail order businesses, yet each one appeals to a different purchaser group and relies upon its own specialized marketing plan.

Direct marketing is especially alluring if you're promotionally minded. The emphasis is not so much on the product but on *selling* the product. And new products are always emerging like ripe plums—to be plucked by promoters who can convert the public's latest fancy into a money-making campaign. Moonlighters can enter a new market quickly and leave it just as fast when profits begin to fade or when heavily capitalized operators move in.

Another attraction of direct marketing is that it eliminates traditional selling costs that even wholesalers must face: rent, payroll, handling, and shrinkage. The store's break-even level of sales goes relentlessly up because of the pressure of utilities, insurance, and other fixed costs. Payroll costs are ballooning because of higher minimum wages, workers' compensation insurance, and Social Security withholdings. Direct marketing is free of these expenses.

Once you learn the ropes, you can build a direct-marketing business faster than would be possible in any retail store. The retail store depends on patronage, which takes time to build up; but a hot mail order campaign can be *faxed* into an advertising medium with one phone call.

Direct marketing also offers the advantage of income tax deferral. Since the major expense for the direct marketer is the advertising bill, these up-front costs are treated as expenses. If you're into direct marketing in a permanent way, advertising expended today will create sales continuing into future years. And your advertising expenses will shelter your early earnings from income taxes. The net result is you will have much more cash to expand the business as you get the hang of what, where, and how to sell.

If you operate a retail business, direct marketing can be deployed to supplement your over-the-counter sales. It could make the difference between success or failure in a marginal retail operation. Here are some examples:

- A struggling gift shop simply hangs up a sign: "We mail anywhere in the world." These additional incremental sales add mightily to overall profits.
- The restaurant industry has increased the emphasis on "food to go" business.
- A successful curio shop increased its sales 25 percent by circulating a mail-order catalog. Their mailing list consisted of highly qualified buyers: their own customers. Their average mail-order sale was $40, while the average sale in the store by walk-in customers was $12.
- Wright Shoe Company, a financial turnaround, supplemented their sales to retail stores with a direct-mail program.

Another unique advantage in direct marketing is you can test market a product before committing yourself to sell it. Retail merchants opening a new location cannot be sure that the location will be a good one. But through copycatting and testing, you'll have a good idea of what an advertising campaign can produce in sales and profits—before running it at full throttle.

Direct marketing is surely an activity for those who enjoy advertising, because this is the heart of the matter. It is not uncommon for direct-mail companies to create in-house advertising agencies in order to eliminate the 17 percent markup normally charged. Some of the large direct-mail companies spend 60 percent of their total revenue on advertising; these fees become a significant factor. To avoid this expense, you can set up your own in-house agency of a caliber acceptable to most media sellers. This know-how can be picked up from direct-marketing literature.

Direct marketing should have special appeal for women moonlighters. More and more of the great entrepreneurial success stories concern women who have forged ahead on their own in full-time or moonlight businesses. But many women are still homemakers and do not have the opportunity to fully express their business talents; direct marketing offers the possibility to do so. This playing field requires only intellectual agility and the willingness to patiently follow proven techniques.

Direct-marketing opportunities that did not exist a decade ago are now blossoming. Without the constraints of operating a store, you can ship products out of your house to any location via private delivery systems—all managed in moonlight hours. You can start from scratch with a minimum of capital. And in fact, you *should* start small, part time, with a toe-in-the-water-first approach.

But now let's look at some of the disquieting aspects of starting a direct-marketing company. On the surface it would appear to be a business where innovative merchandising is the key to success. It is not. To sell profitably in direct marketing requires specialized knowledge, disciplined regimentation, and a willingness to follow in the footsteps of pioneers who have paved the way.

If your first advertising campaigns do not draw customers, you're capital is going to blow away. You'll be burned out before even getting started. The painful truth is that the winners are not so much the leaders as they are the followers; they are the statisticians, not the hot-shot salespeople.

The moonlighter must also carefully weigh other potential problems. The elimination of rent, employees, and all the other expenses carry with them a singular drawback: since customers don't come into the store, you must go out and find them. Direct marketing must get the attention of the passive buyer and at the same time create an instantaneous decision to buy. This must all be accomplished by advertising—which is *enormously* expensive to do effectively. The truth is that direct marketing is a very expensive way to conduct business.

This single, crushing expense of advertising represents much much more than what retailers will ever spend on rent and clerks. Rent expense might, for instance, represent ten percent of sales, but direct marketing advertising can easily be thirty percent to fifty percent. Therefore, direct-marketed merchandise cannot generally compete on a price basis with merchandise sold over the counter, because the retailer can operate with a lower margin of profit than can the direct marketer.

As direct-marketing expert Julian Simon observes, "It is not a business to be run with the left hand, from a hammock and between fishing trips." And there's no such thing as an ongoing dream product. A good direct-marketed product will only have a limited time to sell profitably because, with success, competition will swarm in.

Direct marketing will be disappointing for moonlighters who crave outlets for their creativity. Notoriously, exciting new products do not sell especially well through direct marketing. The first rule of the professionals in the business is to never offer a brand new product. Quite the contrary, the recommended path to success is that of the quick-thinking copycat.

It's possible to get into trouble in direct marketing through overzealousness. You won't have the constraints of a retail business, which depends on word-of-mouth and goodwill. Each of your sales is a one-shot deal, and there is a temptation to exaggerate claims. The buyers can't ask questions or examine the merchandise. All they know about it is what your advertising claims, and this increases the chances of your customers being misinformed.

In the past, some direct sellers perpetrated outrageous scams. These days few dare to try, because there are a host of federal and state agencies to persecute the unscrupulous operator. The U.S. postal service, the Federal Trade Commission, the FDA, and various state agencies all have the power to stop, fine, and jail delinquent business people. For those who don't actually land in jail, it is rarely worth the expense of defending dubious products in court.

Direct marketing requires that you be a patient and analytical person. Most go into business in order to become leaders, not followers. But self-expression in direct marketing is limited to finding out what already works and does not allow for making leadership decisions or devising new products. But playing poker is not a creative activity either, but it can be very satisfying—provided one is good enough to win consistently.

If you're interested in seriously looking into becoming a direct-market moonlighter, here are some suggestions on how to begin. First of all, I recommend Julian Simon's book, *How To Start and Operate A Mail Order Business* (McGraw-Hill, New York, New York, 1981). If nothing else, you will discover that there's a lot to be learned: strategies, product decisions, cost analysis, display and classified advertising techniques, how to write ad copy, and a great deal more.

The "me too" principle is the recommended approach for the start-up moonlighter genuinely interested in mail order. To begin with, you have no reason to risk your financial resources for trial-and-error experimentation. Let those who are already in the game do the experimenting. The starting problem is that you don't know what has already been tried and failed. Copycatting works because you can study what is selling by tracking the ads of competitors. A picture will emerge revealing the successful products.

In traditional retailing you can observe everything the competition is doing because it's in the open: the store, the prices, and the marketing techniques. In direct marketing there's only one window into the competition's operation: their advertising. Unless you know what is selling, and how it is advertised, you are in the dark.

Careful research into the advertising used by others will disclose exactly what items are moving. If you study enough media advertising, the ads will become familiar to you, and you'll know whom to emulate. Eventually you'll realize that there are relatively few successful products and even fewer successful firms. The bottom line is to let the predecessor, your competition, bear the cost of testing and finally targeting a successful product—and then copy it.

Since advertising is by far the greatest expense, the success or failure of a new undertaking will depend entirely on whether sufficient sales can be generated to cover the cost of reaching the customer. When your research has determined a likely product, you can test your product before laying down the big bet. Direct marketing is a calculated operation of experiment and feedback rather than a random game of chance.

Author Julian Simon tells about his own start-up in the mail-order business. He had a fine background in advertising and a doctorate in business economics. In order to determine what to sell, he read every available book and talked with everyone he could find who knew something on the subject. He finally went full steam ahead with four major product lines. Doesn't this sound as if he was perfectly prepared? It was a complete bust. Self-expression in direct marketing can be very expensive. More bluntly, innovators get killed.

What he *did* learn was that his education availed him naught in learning the secret of what he calls "The Professional Method." His secret is simply that direct marketing does not reward new ideas: the chances of failure are overwhelming when you market any new product. What works is tirelessly copycatting what has already been proven to be successful. You even use the same media as the competition—because that's where the payout has been proven.

There are other skills which must also be mastered: locating your sources of supply, dexterity in handling mail, shipping options, and competence in computer technology—all these are necessary. Computers will be essential for managing your records. Personal computers have become so powerful, and the software packages so versatile, that you will have all the capacity you will ever need.

Young moonlighters accept the computer as a standard tool because the technology was part of their learning process in school. It is the older entrepreneur who must break down the inhibitions and learn PC technology. Courses are offered in extension classes, but the most direct solution is to plug the machine in and turn it on. When you make a mistake, it will politely inform you.

Here are some product lines that have been successfully sold by direct marketing: food, health and medical products, cosmetics, clothing, jewelry, books, courses offered by correspondence schools, information services, photography, art, toys, printing, economic newsletters, local services, and hobbies. The list could go on and on.

One overall theme I have stressed is that the moonlighter should learn a chosen business by first going to work for someone else in the same line of work. In direct marketing it may not be practical to work for someone else, so it's necessary to learn the business by reading about the experience of others. Devour everything you can get your hands on.

The "how-to" books on this subject make interesting reading. You will find hundreds of case stories about what works and what doesn't. The literature on how to write advertising copy is also fascinating, because those who write on the subject are interesting personalities in their own right, as well as expert advisors. It is all laid out for you—in print.

And it doesn't take the gift of gab. There's no requirement to be an articulate glad-hander to win out in this business. This may be especially appealing to the introverted moonlighter who is not possessed with an outgoing personality. In fact, direct marketing does have a potential element of loneliness about it. But it's a fascinating business for the methodical person and offers everyone, even the most timid individual, the exhilarating experience of running a sideline business.

CHAPTER SIXTEEN

# Serve People

The he shrewd moonlighter should be where the action is. Here is one such place: of the twelve million jobs created since the 1981–82 recession, nearly 80 percent have been in services. Service businesses now deliver paychecks to 70 percent of all workers in the private sector. Nine out of ten new jobs during the nineties will be in service industries. In this chapter I will point to some ways you can moonlight by serving people.

First, the big picture. The Bureau of Labor Statistics divides the economy into two sectors. One is called goods-producing: farming, mining, construction, and manufacturing. The other, the service-producing sector, includes literally everything else. Starting about 1970, jobs in manufacturing began to dwindle and during recession years fell into a tailspin.

Manufacturing jobs are vanishing for two reasons. One is that manufacturing has undergone impressive gains in productivity. The other reason is the loss of American manufacturing jobs to overseas producers. In 1980, output was one-third greater than in 1970, but employment had only increased 5 percent. It's the same story already played out in agriculture: farm production today only requires 4 percent of the country's work force compared with 60 percent in 1860.

These gains in farming and manufacturing efficiency have permitted us to provide services a poorer society could not afford such as fine restaurants, leisure and health-oriented activities, and more sophisticated health care. The jobs created by these service industries have taken up the slack in manufacturing.

McDonald's alone now has 400,000 employees! For most of the eight million former "crew people," Big Mac offered a start rather than a career. McDonald's honored its former employees in a television ad campaign that included a profile of a woman who began frying burgers as a teenager to pay for her contact lenses. She is still in the service business—as an ophthalmologist.

The following table may offer you some clues as to where the opportunities are. According to the Department of Labor, the ten occupations that will supply the largest number of jobs through 1995 are *all* in services. None of them are high-tech, yet plenty of opportunity will also open up for lawyers and other trained professionals. This is the forecast:

| Job | 1984–1995 Increase |
|---|---|
| Cashiers | 556,000 |
| Registered nurses | 452,000 |
| Janitors and cleaners | 443,000 |
| Truck drivers | 428,000 |
| Waiters and waitresses | 424,000 |
| Wholesale trade sales workers | 369,000 |
| Nursing aides, orderlies | 348,000 |
| Retail salespersons | 343,000 |
| Accountants and auditors | 307,000 |
| Teachers (elementary) | 281,000 |

Some economists predict that a service economy must count on sales to basic industries to survive. Major manufacturers are now harnessing links to a wide network of service companies ranging from advertising agencies to financial concerns. General Motor's largest single supplier is now not a steel company but Blue Cross. And there are as many people now working in car dealerships as those who work in auto manufacturing. Manufacturers are subcontracting services they once supplied themselves—not merely janitorial work but also highly paid positions in legal, accounting, and consulting departments as well.

Lynda Falkenstein conducts "Consulting For Profit" seminars coast to coast and now counts her attendees in the thousands. Bankers, managers, engineers, business brokers, real estate professionals, and others are all interested in getting into consulting practices. According to Dr. Falkenstein, the 1987 median income for consulting professionals exceeded $90,000.

The shift to services hasn't meant that we're producing fewer goods. Manufacturing has consistently maintained a forty-six percent share of the GNP for more than two decades. If America can turn out the same amount of goods with fewer workers, then this simply means that we have become more efficient. We have developed an economy with more disposable income for purchasing new and better services. Perhaps the boom in services is a reflection of what is *good* about the U.S. economy rather than what is bad.

In starting up your own moonlight business, the decision to be in service or manufacturing is not as important as selecting a field of growth rather than a stagnant one. Lower birth rates since the sixties have resulted in a baby bust that will reduce the need for college professors, but training centers will be needed to keep technicians up to date. So forget the Ph.D. in Sanskrit and start a trade school to teach computer programming instead.

Here are eight service categories that in my opinion offer moon-lighters a wide assortment of possibilities. Your opportunity could lie in:

- ▸ Filling emerging personal needs
- ▸ Satisfying the drive for personal health
- ▸ Helping with yard or household chores
- ▸ Working in the import/export business
- ▸ Retailing and distribution
- ▸ Informing people—there's lots of information out there!
- ▸ Starting a business in leisure, travel, or entertainment
- ▸ Solving the emerging complexities of modern life

Let's look at some specific examples. "Emerging personal needs" refers to services that didn't exist in the past. There was a time when you wouldn't think of closing your front door, let alone dead-bolting it shut—but not these days. Our homes have become the targets of maraud-ing burglars who must satisfy their expensive habits. The greeting "mi casa es su casa" has taken on a sinister new meaning.

Alongside our "welcome" doormats are signs announcing: "Acme Security Systems, ARMED RESPONSE." These signs are no hollow de-terrent. Homes are rigged with sophisticated devices to detect forced entry, which are connected to (sometimes independently operated) monitoring stations that dispatch the police and anybody else designated to defend your fortress-home from the depredations of criminals.

For practical reasons, the residential security business didn't exist twenty years ago. Today it offers an expanding opportunity for protecting tens of millions of homes and apartments. For the technically inclined moonlighter, this is a business that won't conflict with your regular job, because both the selling and installation functions can be done after hours. And there is still growth potential here, as crime rates stubbornly refuse to fall.

Another emerging need has been spawned by bank deregulation. Where do workers in casual jobs or service businesses go to cash their paychecks? Not to the banks, which are no longer providing the retailing services for walk-in customers they once did. This need is satisfied by "check cashing services." On the premises you can also obtain money orders for a fraction of what banks charge nonprivileged customers and pick up mail from rented post office boxes.

The increasing fixation on health has spawned all sorts of oppor-tunities. There are more gyms and health food stores because we want to live longer and look younger. According to Tom Fatjo, chairman of LivingWell, a health club chain, fitness is a $35 billion industry, and he claims "we've just scratched the surface." His largest market is not so much the moneyed crowd but rather new members who can only afford $20 a month to work out.

Keeping healthy is more a matter of preventative measures than waiting to be treated for physical ailments as they happen. We're now convinced that wellbeing is a direct function of what we eat and drink, how much we weigh, and how much we exercise. No longer is the stereotypical business tycoon depicted in advertisements as a portly cigar chomper but instead as a trim jock running a ten-kilometer race in Central Park.

For women, being healthy is more than a matter of longevity. A dating-service owner in Boston reports that today's selective singles want partners who are in good health; the hardest people to match are single women who smoke. Since the number of unmarried women exceeds the number of single men (which increases as we age) single women have become a prime target for fitness businesses. This presents opportunity for women moonlighters.

A seedy motel in Palm Springs was ready for the bulldozer but instead was renovated and reopened as a fitness spa. Other newer hotels struggle with marginal occupancy rates; this facility has clients swarming from all parts of the country. Ninety percent of the customers are women who come to tone up, wind down, lose weight, and relax. The spa also spins off supplemental health-related services such as facial treatments, massages, and individual diet consultation. All are paid-for items. This enterprise is run by a woman who started out as a physical education teacher. She no longer rides to work on the bus but arrives in a limousine.

In a more medical vein, Penny Budoff, a physician in Bethpage, New York, guessed correctly that women were ready for a change at the doctor's office. She sensed a widespread feeling among women patients that doctors rushed and patronized them. Penny opened a full-service clinic for women staffed entirely by female internists, radiologists, therapists, and nutritionists.

Her sex-segregated clinic now boasts more than 7,000 patients. She may have been the first, but others are finding that it pays to take the preferences of women patients seriously. Since women spend more on health care than men (by a margin of 25 percent), this remains an enormous, untapped market. Following her example would be a good idea for entrepreneurially inclined women with medical training.

The changing economics of medicine has caused an increase in moonlighting among the growing number of doctors employed by hospitals or HMOs. Competition is increasing because of the forty percent increase in the number of physicians during the last decade and the economic restructuring toward prepaid service. Investor-owned hospitals and clinics are indications of profit motives (and moonlighting opportunities) in the provision of health care.

Yet "staying well" businesses are less in the hands of the medical profession (which has never crusaded for preventive medicine) than of nutritionists, physical culturists (sometimes quacks), and entrepreneurs. Even the treatment of addiction illnesses such as drug or alcohol dependency is more the territory of profit-motivated clinics than of medical doctors. The moonlighter with skills in health care has many opportunities to consider.

Many services are in demand because more adults are working. In fact, more than half the U.S. population is now in the labor force. For the first time ever, there are more workers than dependents. All sorts of services previously performed at home now must be done by someone hired outside the home.

Who has time to walk the dog? Don't laugh—if you think this is a trivial problem, in New York it is not. Poodle-walking is performed by a large number of moonlighters. More important, who is going to take care of the pre-school children while the parents work? In Los Angeles, couples now put their children's names on school waiting lists as soon as the names are chosen.

Having someone clean the house is no longer a luxury but a necessity for working folks. A young trial lawyer I know made gobs of money and retired in Palm Springs, but soon found himself going crazy with boredom. To help decide on a sideline business, he had each of his friends make a list of their most critical and unsatisfied needs. His answer surfaced at once. Everyone he knew had the same #1 problem: finding a good cleaning lady.

He figured this was his opportunity. He recruited hotel maids pleased to moonlight at higher-than-minimum wages. They all start out at his office, where they are provided with smartly tailored smocks. (No pockets—he's a suspicious fellow.) Teams then return to his office before going home; with this arrangement, it's not an easy matter to carry off the crystal. His business was an overnight success.

Sharon Van Tassel of St. Paul, Minnesota, offers a splendid example of someone who started a sideline service business out of her home. Sharon started "Handy Helpers." She got the idea when convalescing from an illness. While daydreaming about going into business, this idea occurred to her: "Why not start a *totally* personal service company?" Her plan was to take on absolutely any personal chore that people were unable to handle themselves.

Her initial investment was fifty dollars for printing up flyers, which she distributed in housing complexes and pinned to grocery store bulletin boards. The response was overwhelming: twenty-two replies for every one hundred flyers sent out! Other than running two ads in the local newspaper, it was the only advertising Sharon ever had to pay for. All she does now is to send thank-you notes and Christmas cards to her clients.

Word-of-mouth does the rest. A selection of her services shows the extent to which working people no longer have the time to perform routine tasks:

▶ Watering plants
▶ Picking up prescriptions
▶ Grocery shopping (for the elderly as well as working people)
▶ Waiting for telephone, gas, electric, or other servicepeople
▶ Opening cans for the handicapped
▶ Housecleaning
▶ Window washing
▶ Preparing food for parties ("cooking and baking")
▶ Christmas shopping
▶ Providing temporary typists and receptionists for businesses
▶ Providing janitorial service for businesses

Sharon has one client who is a woman in a senior management position for a large company. She leaves *everything* to Handy Helpers, including grocery shopping, doing the housecleaning and laundry, cooking meals for company, taking her car in for service, and yard maintenance. Fees for each of these jobs are charged by the hour according to the type of work.

While Sharon now has fifty to sixty people working for her at any given time, she has never put an ad in the newspaper for personnel. She has never had to hire someone she didn't know or who was not referred by someone already working for her. Most are either part-time college students or retired people. One of her employees (who learned about her from the flyer) is a lawyer who washes windows on weekends. For him, it's a form of relaxing exercise!

Sharon's enjoys getting unusual requests. One executive has her pick out and arrange a reservation for him in a different restaurant for each Friday night. She also writes out the checks to pay bills for an old bachelor. It's not out of the ordinary for her to be asked to have someone wait in line for tickets for rock concerts or sporting events.

Other aspects of her business are geared to precisely tuned procedures. Her housecleaning service has become a time and motion study. Crews of three workers can clean four houses in a day by following a systematic routine. Their work includes putting sheets and towels into the washing machine the moment they walk in. The vacuuming, dusting, washing down of kitchen and bathrooms, and cleaning the refrigerator and stove (on the outside only) are all performed by efficient teamwork.

Sharon still runs Handy Helpers out of her home, and much of her services are repeat business. Her biggest sources of income, by order of importance, are:

- Personnel services to businesses
- Housecleaning
- Shopping for groceries
- Gift buying

International trade is yet another possibility for a sideline service business. A friend of mine recently retired from Manville Corp., for which he ran the international division. He has added spice (and income) to his retirement by taking on a line of Japanese Fax machines for distribution throughout his home state of Colorado. This activity can be conducted in hours of his own choosing.

Know-how in the import/export field can be gained from an expanding array of university extension courses. Most extension programs don't require a college degree and range from introductory to advanced classes. For example, in the field of international business, UCLA offers the following courses each year:

Fundamentals of Import Trade
Introduction to International Business
International Finance
International Marketing
Law in International Business
International Business Management
International Economics
Starting Your own Import/Export Business

There are as many service opportunities for retired women as there are for men. When the kids have at last moved out, most women think that they have—at last—attained peace. But today, most are no longer satisfied to stay at home. They want to become entrepreneurs! My wife, her two best friends, and my sister-in-law are all at that point in life, and each one of them has opted to go into a moonlight business. Peggy, as you know by now, is marketing her squeegee and developing shopping centers.

Judi Weiseman is a Los Angeles school teacher who recently started a sideline calligraphy business. She first scouted the greeting card shops to decide which card companies to represent. Once she was set up, she began placing orders directly to the factories. Judi sells wedding invitations, general announcements, and customized stationery—all of which are selected from her sample books. Most of her referrals come from a local catering hall used for parties and bar mitzvahs.

She can spend as much or as little time at her moonlighting as she wants. As it is, she is perfectly satisfied to handle three or four orders a month with no advertising at all. But if she wanted to build up her business, she would begin to advertise in the local papers.

It's now possible to produce calligraphy on CAD (computer-assisted design) computers, which are making inroads into this business. Rather than sending orders to printers on the East Coast, personalized invitations are produced on equipment that is ITSB (in the spare bedroom). One lady paid $8,000 for such a machine and opened a business in San Marino, California. Operating out of her home, she paid for the machine in four months.

Daina Johnson was an elementary school teacher before going into business. During a period of ten years she has built her venture, Tudor Cottage, into an extremely successful gift shop in La Cañada, California. She has the flair for buying just the right merchandise and displaying it attractively. She was also astute enough to buy a "trademark" old English-style house, situated in a commercial zone, for her business. Over the years, the property has skyrocketed in value.

From the profits of this business, Daina bought herself *another* Tudor cottage at Lake Arrowhead, California, as a get-away home. There she started a second (shall we say moonlight) business: "Dog Ear'd Books." To launch it, she purchased 12,000 used paperback books for ten cents apiece. Her source was a lady who runs a similar operation, "Paperback Exchange," in Reno, Nevada.

Customers bring in two used paperbacks and trade them for one paperback already displayed in the store. Of course, the customer can also purchase a used paperback, usually for one-half the jacket price. After one year in business, Daina has built her inventory up from 12,000 to 18,000 books, while at the same time donating many to charitable organizations. Although she runs a weekly ad in the local newspaper, the bulk of her business is now attributed to word of mouth.

Anita Revill opened a gift shop in the Topanga Plaza Mall in Woodland Hills, California. She was assisted by her husband, Jim, who meanwhile continues in his full-time job. For him it was a moonlight operation; for her it was a switch from a job as a doctor's office manager. The shop is only 600 square feet, but during the Christmas buying season Anita requires as many as five clerks to handle the business. The gifts are for the most part personalized with the names of the eventual recipients.

And speaking of the power of personalization, I was window shopping last Christmas and spotted a toy store displaying Christmas stockings with a sign, "Name Imprinted Free." I purchased eight as place settings for a party we were planning. The imprinting was simple. A salesgirl "wrote" out each name in glue on the stockings, then dipped them into a box of glitter. The sale was made because they provided a *personalized* service.

Another expanding field is communications. The *Los Angeles Business Journal* publishes a "Book of Lists" that tabulates the top southern California companies. Under the heading of "Cellular Car Phone Distributors," seventeen of the top twenty-five firms didn't even *exist* before 1983!

If you're already into computers and data handling, keep in mind that half of the electronic information sold in the United States is used by financial institutions and stock market players. (E.F. Hutton has spent about $100 million on this alone during the past eight years.) This leaves a great number of untapped prospects.

The biggest opportunities will be in targeting statistics that can be conveniently databased and sold to firms that can in turn realize competitive advantages with the information. Urban Decision Systems packages demographic data for chain stores, which pay them annual fees amounting to the thousands of dollars.

In the past, deciding on new store locations was a purely subjective judgment based on traffic counts and other factors—including gut feelings. Recently, computer site models have been devised by software firms specializing in this field. The primary source of the data used is the U.S. census, but Urban Decisions has organized the information in a way that would be prohibitively expensive for any single user to duplicate.

Can you think of a way to package useful information and sell it to different customers? Metromail Co. repackages its consumer-household database into nearly a dozen different products and sells them to publishers, catalog companies, and market researchers. Corporations will pay just about any price for proprietary strategic information. Your success will depend upon pinpointing paying markets. And as businesses take more advantage of sophisticated information sources, furnishing information could turn into a major industry in its own right.

Leisure and travel offer alluring possibilities to moonlighters who like to travel. Why not become an expert in a specialized line and advertise as such? The January 1989 issue of *Fortune* reported that the number of Americans who file up the gangplanks of cruise ships has gone up 600% since 1980. Ocean cruises are no longer a diversion for the nearly dead; such travel ventures now enjoy a market of 150 million people who up to now have taken vacations in hotels. A prominent minister I know moonlights by conducting tours to New England and other destinations worldwide. Many of his clients are his parishioners.

Another opportunity for service moonlighting is to help people solve the increasing complexities of modern life. We tend to lag in our ability to cope. If something breaks down, we often stall before getting it fixed. For the individual it's vexing, but the entrepreneur should state it as an equation: Complexity = Opportunity. Some examples:

▶ Toxic and hazardous materials are complicating our lives. UCLA offers a certification program for those interested in the safe containment, handling, and disposal of these materials.

▶ Federal tax legislation has made preparation of personal tax returns a matter for specialists and computers.

▶ Pension planning is no longer a matter of simple choices; it requires the hiring of experts.

▶ The things we use in our daily lives are not built simply anymore. When they malfunction, they're not easy to fix. Must we be ripped off every time we go into a car dealership for an oil change? ("Sorry, your shocks are gone. . . . ") If you like to fix a particular device you may have the basis for serving people.

Moonlighters can succeed by serving people even in the midst of recession. This can happen anywhere. *The Wall Street Journal* issue of July 29, 1991, contained a front page article headed "Business Boomlet— If this is a recession, some people in Poland want even more of it." The entrepreneurs in Poland haven't waited for foreign aid nor do they know that, according to statistics, there is a depression. They have opened pizzerias, dress shops, and grocery stores. "Far into the night they are painting away the drabness of four dismal decades."

And service business is not necessarily small business. The advertising agency of Foote, Cone & Belding bills more than a quarter billion dollars from their Los Angeles office alone (which has 350 employees). Even before merging with Price Waterhouse in 1989, the accounting firm of Arthur Andersen & Co. had no less than 800 CPAs in southern California.

All this should not be seen as a sign of national decay; rather, it's an indication of new opportunities. Sure, there are more hotels and amusement parks, but not because we have become a nation of idlers; we now enjoy greater mobility and more leisure time. The new armies of accountants are not hired to count the beans but to keep abreast of complex government rules.

Your choices are endless. Where are the best overall opportunities? I would suggest you combine the following criteria:

▶ Do something you enjoy.

▶ Fill an expanding need. (The first video store on the block did, but the fifth one did not.)

▶ Save your customer time and travel. (We don't buy bikes anymore, just a package of parts.)

▶ Find a business you will feel good about promoting.

▶ Personalize your product line or service.

Has the service segment become oversaturated? I don't think so. We actually had access to more service in the past than we have today. When did you last have a plumber do a job on the weekend and be glad to get the work? When did you last get service in a "service" station? The cover story of the *Time Magazine* issue of February 2, 1987, was titled, "Pul-eeze! Will Somebody Help Me?" Their conclusion was that personal service has become a maddeningly rare commodity in the American marketplace.

A final how-to example of service is Nordstrom department stores. As other chains cut services to reduce cost, Nordstrom has trained their salesclerks to do quite the opposite. An executive called the Seattle store recently to order a basket of fruit. The store didn't carry them, but in classic Nordstrom fashion the clerk found a specialty shop that did and arranged to have it send the basket. Nordstrom has outperformed virtually every other class-act department store chain in America. You can *remove yourself from competition* with this kind of dedication to service. And you can do it in any business, at any size, in any place you choose.

Thomas Peters, on behalf of all the frustrated consumers who wonder where the service went, said it best: "In general, service in America stinks." This declaration may be your opportunity to become a service industry moonlighter. And this leads me to believe that the dawn is just breaking for those who want to serve people.

# Do Business with the Government

To succeed as a moonlighter, you must engage in something that is assuredly and irrepressibly expanding in its scope. Your own home town probably falls within this definition, and the name of the moonlighter's game is privatization. Since this can be good pickins', let's look into the possibilities.

Privatization is the contracting of services normally performed by government to private individuals and organizations. You would expect that government agencies could underbid private companies because they don't have to make a profit or pay taxes. But it never works out that way. Private businesses are beginning to provide more and more services that formerly were regarded as the exclusive territory of civil workers. Cities and towns find that private contractors can get things done more efficiently and at the same time cut costs by 30 percent or more.

In the past, many political bodies were prohibited by law from contracting out their responsibilities. Before 1979, nearly all services performed by Los Angeles County were required by charter to be furnished by County personnel: for example, maintenance, landscaping, auditing, medical exams, embalming, security, drug testing, and food service. But in 1978, voters passed a landmark amendment permitting the County to contract with private business to perform these and other services. It opened the doors for private enterprise to bid their services in competition with city departments.

Throughout the 1980s, local governments have had to deal with increasing costs and simultaneous cutbacks in federal and state funds. Not only are costs increasing, but service demands as well. The only choices are to increase taxes, cut services, or perform the services at lower costs. This is where privatization comes into play. Cities are learning that private companies can save them money.

In addition to using privatization contracts, which replace services done in the past by city workers, all cities now routinely purchase enormous amounts of goods. The County of Los Angeles purchasing agent annually awards more than $360 million in purchase orders for items ranging from aerial photographs to tires! These purchasing and contracting programs are not only large in dollar amounts, but are also very broad in scope, comprising an enormous variety of goods and services. According to the County's Guide to Vendors, "We do business with giant firms and also with small businesses and individual entrepreneurs."

If you think that really big government only exists at the federal level, consider this: Los Angeles County (a separate entity from the City of Los Angeles and eighty-three other incorporated cities located within the county) has 75,000 *employees* and operates on an annual budget of more than $9 *billion*. But the marketplace for you, the moonlighter, is in the cities that up to now have depended upon county agencies to provide them services.

Privatization, while not new, made momentous gains in the 1980s. Local governments across the country are now turning to private contractors. According to The Reason Foundation, during the ten-year period between 1973 and 1982, contracting work to the private sector increased from 43 percent for refuse collection to 3,644 percent for data processing.

With the potential for savings of this magnitude, it is not surprising that a growing number of cities are resorting to private sources to supply major services. Of the cities and counties that responded to a 1987 Touche Ross survey, the following percentage of them reported contracting out the following services in the last five years:

| | |
|---|---|
| Administrative services | 36% |
| Building/grounds services | 43% |
| Data processing | 31% |
| Vehicle maintenance | 21% |
| Solid waste collection | 69% |
| Street and road services | 29% |

The federal government has been the slowest to respond because of resistance from powerful unions and the political clout of millions of federal civil servants. But small city governments (our moonlighting territory) have embraced privatization because their tax base has eroded through tax reform legislation (such as Proposition 13 in California) and by cutbacks in federal revenue sharing programs.

Government has become uncompetitive by paying more than necessary, especially for low-skilled employees such as custodians and gardeners. Also, civil servants enjoy relatively more fringe benefits including vacations, holidays, and sick leaves. While contractors pay bottom dollar in labor-intensive jobs, they use better equipment and higher-skilled workers on capital-intensive jobs. Also, productivity and hours worked are not as high in the government. The result is that entrepreneurs are providing a greater variety of efficient services.

Some services (such as building and safety) experience peaks and valleys of workload. But cities find it hard to fire employees when they're not needed. Private contractors, on the other hand, can flexibly serve a varying demand. If four engineers are needed, they put on four. If eight are needed, they put on eight.

Historically, small towns have purchased services from the counties they are located in. But bright city managers who in the past routinely contracted with their county government are realizing that their cities are getting fleeced when it comes to costs. So local contractors are being asked to compete with county agencies for providing services.

The entrepreneurs are winning out. Gary Sloan, City Manager of La Mirada, California, couldn't purchase animal control services from either Los Angeles County or the Humane Society (the only resources available to him) because neither had convenient facilities to take on the responsibility. So he encouraged the creation of a privately funded district to handle the job in his (and five other) neighboring cities.

The two Sullivan brothers in Los Angeles had learned from experience that the most effective deterrent to the spread of graffiti was to have it removed the moment after it appeared. They also know that most cities couldn't cope with graffiti problems. By demonstrating that they could handle the job faster (and cheaper) than public works departments, they carved out a successful privatization business.

Andy Lazzaretto realized that small cities don't have the staff to implement redevelopment agency opportunities, and he now represents six cities as a consultant to manage redevelopment projects.

The city of Alhambra recently gave up on its inefficient building department and took RFPs (requests for proposals) from engineering contractors to assume their former responsibilities. Private firms were asked to bid on taking over the functions of building and safety, including plan-checking and building inspection. The RFP also provided that the about-to-be displaced employees would be interviewed (but not necessarily hired) by the contractor. The successful bidder was Willdan Associates and after meetings with the former staff, they agreed with the city management: Willdan had no use for them either.

What kind of firms do business with local governments? How Willdan got its start will give some idea. In 1964 Dan Heil, its founder, was an engineer for the City of Fullerton in California. When he decided to fire an incompetent employee, his boss was horrified. And in dead earnest he was told that incompetence at work *wasn't* a sufficient cause. His boss said, "You can't do that!"

Heil didn't want to spend a career playing that game. He quit and set himself up as a private engineer with the intention of contracting with small cities as a plan checker. He started out in a trailer with a single account, the rapidly growing city of Dairy Valley. Heil's job was to do exactly what he had been doing at Fullerton. Only now he was an entrepreneur, on his own time and *in charge* of the hiring and firing of his employees. No longer was he obligated to keep someone on the payroll if they weren't doing their job competently.

While there are certain functions that government is reluctant to privatize (notably police and fire protection), entrepreneurs are providing many other services more cheaply than governments can. In 1983 Los Angeles County contracted out the food service in the USC Medical Center. Of the 200 county employees in the facility, 100 went with the contractor and in some instances received higher pay. By 1986 the contractor was saving the county a cool $1.8 million annually, and both service and quality of food had been substantially improved.

Private contractors can demonstrate the kind of ingenuity that never occurs to unmotivated civil servants. The firm that took over parking at the Los Angeles Music Center increased county revenues in a number of innovative ways:

▸ The addition of valet parking ($100,000/year)
▸ The addition of monthly parking ($100,000/year)
▸ The conversion of "sacred cow" parking for performers and stagehands to stacked parking plus public parking ($300,000/year)

Later, the acute shortage of downtown parking was made worse by the loss of 400 car spaces to the newly planned Metrorail station. The same contractor consequently moved these cars over to the Music Center and ingeniously devised a plan of stacking them to provide the additional spaces.

There are many entry points for the moonlighter to take over public services. Listed here are some of the typical functions that have already been successfully handled by private business:

| | |
|---|---|
| Engineering | Golf course operation |
| Trash removal | Legal services |
| Street maintenance | Airport control towers |
| Landscape maintenance | Janitorial services |
| Feeding | Hospital operation |
| Jails/detention centers | Soil decontamination/toxic waste removal |
| School buses | Animal control |
| Police protection | Traffic signal maintenance |
| Dial-a-ride services | Accounting |

| | |
|---|---|
| Consulting services | City management |
| Weed abatement | Embalming |
| Parking lots | Towing |
| Travel services | Temporary office help |

Virtually every department in the County of Los Angeles has begun to contract out some of its functions. Pages 130 and 131 show exactly what services each department has already delegated to private firms. This represents only the beginning of what is a civic revolution. The following services are under examination for *future* privatization:

| **Service** | **Possibilities** |
|---|---|
| Inmate medical service: | Potential extra income for start-up physicians to pay off education loans |
| Pre-employment medical: | Same as above |
| Management of vehicle fleets: | Entire bus systems are now open-season for privatization |
| Investigative service: | Appropriate for moonlighting or retired law enforcement officers |
| Document serving: | Same as above |
| Nursery services: | An opportunity for women moon-lighters |
| Risk management: | For the insurance expert wishing to vent the entrepreneurial urge |
| Work measurement (productivity): | Consultants will begin to replace bureaucrats in special-knowledge and high-tech activities |

The bottom line is that you must show your city how to save money. This is best done by not privatizing on a piecemeal basis but instead in big chunks. To help evaluate whether your proposal is cost effective, a bid is also submitted by the department previously responsible for the service. You must demonstrate true savings, defined as costs that actually disappear. When officials calculate the local authority's bid, overhead costs that do not go away are excluded. In such instances your bid must then compete with costs that do not provide for government overhead.

This is why it's better not to privatize piecemeal, where related overhead still has to be carried on as before. Instead, you can show greater savings by contracting out the whole service and thereby eliminating struc-

Departmental Privatization Contracting by Service Areas

| Department | Service Area | Appeals repr. | Audit | Building Mgmt. | Collection | Custodial | Data Conversion | Dietary | Embalming | Equipment Repair | Golf Course Ops. |
|---|---|---|---|---|---|---|---|---|---|---|---|
| Arboreta | | | | | | | | | | | |
| Auditor–Controller | | | X | | | | | | | | |
| Beaches and Harbors | | | X | | | | | | | | |
| Chief Admin. Office | | | | | | | | | | | |
| Chf. Med. Exam–Coroner | | | | | | | | | X | | |
| Children's Services | | | | | | X | | | | | |
| Co. Clerk/Superior Court | | | | | | | | | | | |
| Community & Sr. Cit. | | | | | | | | | | | |
| County Counsel | | | | | | | | | | | |
| Data Processing | | | | | | | X | | | | |
| Facilities Management | | | | X | | X | | | | | |
| Forester and Fire Warden | | | | | | | | | | X | |
| Health Services | | | | | | | | X | | | |
| Museum of Art | | | | | | X | | | | | |
| Museum of Nat. History | | | | | | X | | | | | |
| Parks and Recreation | | | | | | | | | | | X |
| Probation | | | | | | | | X | | | |
| Public Library | | | | | | X | | | | | |
| Public Social Services | | X | | | | | | | | | |
| Public Works | | | | | | | | | | | |
| Purchasing and Stores | | | | | | | | | | | |
| Treas. and Tax Collector | | | | | X | | | | | | |

tured overhead. For example, Los Angeles County is now considering whether to eliminate its entire airport division by transferring this function to private enterprise.

In another example from Los Angeles County, the overall operation of printing is under study. Each department presently has its own print shop for a total of eleven separate shops. By replacing all of them with a single outside contractor, the associated overhead would disappear and the savings would be much more favorable.

| Laboratory Tests | Landscape Maint. | Laundry | Liab. Claim. Mgmt. | Med. Fee Review | Mgmt. Training | Microfilming | Parking | Records Storage | Referral Service | Secretarial | Security | Towing | Transcribing | Transportation | Travel Service |
|---|---|---|---|---|---|---|---|---|---|---|---|---|---|---|---|
| X | | | | | | | | | | | | | | | |
| | | | | | | | | | | | | | | | X |
| X | | | | | | | X | | | | X | | | X | |
| | | | X | | | | | | | | | | | | |
| | | | | | | | | | | | | | | | |
| X | | | | | | | | | | | | | | | |
| | | | | | | X | | | | X | | | | | |
| | | | | | | | | | | | | | | X | |
| | | X | | | | | | | | | | | | | |
| | | | | | | | | | | | | | | | |
| | | | | | | | X | | | | X | X | | | |
| | | | | | | | | | | | | | | | |
| | X | X | | | | | | | | | X | | X | | |
| | | | | | | | | | | | X | | | | |
| | | | | | | | | | | | X | | | | |
| X | | | | | | | | | | | X | | | | |
| X | | | | | | | | | | | | | X | | |
| | X | | | | | | | | | | | | | | |
| | | | | X | | | | X | X | | | | | | |
| X | X | | | | | | | | | | X | | | | |
| | | | | | | | | | | | X | | | | |
| | | | | | | | | | | | | | | | |

If you're interested in a privatization business, you must scrupulously follow the criteria set forth by the government. In some cases, Los Angeles County bases 10 percent of their overall evaluation on how the contractor provides for rehiring displaced employees. This can easily be overlooked by an overly eager bidder. Also, your chances are enhanced by designing a highly innovative proposal that would be difficult to get anywhere else. If you have an original technique for carrying out a government program, explore the possibility with the appropriate department.

Doing business with the government (even in small towns) will carry some tough compromises. You will be deferring to, and in some measure submitting to, the whims of entrenched bureaucratic office holders who may feel that you're a threat to their security. It won't be quite the same as wheeling and dealing with a hard-nosed, motivated customer to convince him or her that your deal is better than your competitor's. Bear in mind that your contacts will be with those who cannot be fired and that civil servants have become the acknowledged masters of the art of nurturing bureaucratic empires.

This touchy aspect highlights the inherent inefficiencies of public monopolies. By taking work out of the public sector, you really do threaten the bureaucrat's prized power. To defend against this threat, civil servants are not always civil when dealing with contractors. The public sector may now have to depend more on private firms but is not about to have their security diminished in so doing. As a contractor, you will be contending with rules ingeniously designed to maintain power firmly in the hands of officialdom. When you are asked to jump, be prepared to swallow your pride and ask, "How high?"

The system of letting out contracts has been designed so as to permit the government agency to make its own complex evaluation of the bidders, rather than be locked into the lowest (and perhaps least qualified) bidder. Leery officials, referring to carefully worded standards, can select "the most promising all-around bidder" and not necessarily the one lowest in price. Here are the criteria you can expect them to use. You must:

- Have adequate financial resources to carry out contract commitments.
- Be able to comply with delivery requirements.
- Have a satisfactory record in performing similar tasks.
- Have a satisfactory record of integrity.
- Be able to secure adequate insurance and in some cases bonding.

Most government bodies require substantial vendor capability as well as two or more years of experience in providing similar services. If you have the ability to deal with the bureaucratic process but don't have the specific experience needed, perhaps you could team up with someone who does. At the same time, your partner could be the one responsible for the day-to-day management while you're at your job.

If you're a professional moonlighter, you may have an easier time in starting up than otherwise, because your credentials are already in place. For example a lawyer, CPA, or doctor can all readily establish their professional authenticity. In looking through the breakdown of County contracts, "consulting" comes up again and again, which makes me think this is an especially good opportunity for qualified moonlighters.

My advice is to start out as modestly as possible just to get launched. The goal is to establish that first beachhead, as Dan Heil did in Dairy Valley. As an inexperienced moonlighter just getting started, you're not going to get your first contract in a big government body.

But for the heavy hitters, some areas are less crowded by virtue of the high capital investment required, such as busing. I am told that even in the huge southern California market, private street sweeping is still something of a monopoly because of high equipment costs. Wherever you aim, remember that there are some troublesome spots you should watch for:

- Insurance requirements will be tough. You will need an insurance agent who has good connections with bonding companies. (A faithful performance bond will be required where contractor default might create a financial risk for the agency.)
- Contractors can be fired. There are normally no tenure guarantees. The City of La Mirada's Dial-a-Ride contract was so novel as to be cited by *Time* magazine as an example of creative privatization. Yet after six months of poor service, City Manager Gary Sloan finally discharged the firm. Moral: You've got to do a good job, and keep doing it.
- There *can* be political implications, especially in smaller jurisdictions. The voters of Hawaiian Gardens in Orange County elected an entirely new City Council. The new members immediately replaced competent operating contractors with new ones of their own choice. Yet the methods used by government agencies in privatizing are by and large fair and open to all.

You can look to a number of sources for business, including the sale of goods and services that the agencies have always purchased from outside vendors. Normally, the types of government business are broken down as follows:

- Purchase of goods and specialized services.
- Concession contracts, to manage services such as parking lots (in Los Angeles County, twelve out of eighteen golf courses are contracted. These contracts can be for as long as twenty-five years).
- Design and construction of capital projects (perhaps not a territory for moonlighters).
- Privatization of services now performed by government.
- Leasing of property (for real estate moonlighters).

My own home town, La Habra Heights, provides some examples of where to begin. First of all, it's small, boasting a total population under

6,000. City Manager Bob Gutierrez advises that the best place for the moonlighter to start is the City Manager's office. Simply walk in, ask what types of work are contracted out, and offer your services. You may then be referred to another department, but at least you are assured of getting the right information to begin with.

Such small municipalities cannot justify much in the way of staff and may have depended on county agencies, but counties tend to be easy competition. This is proven out in La Habra Heights by the number of services that are nowadays *not* done by the county, including building and safety, engineering, weed control, and even the fire department. The county is losing out to local contractors who can prove that they are not only lower in cost but can do a better job.

The large agencies, however, can give you a better feel of the ropes. Los Angeles County publishes a comprehensive booklet entitled, "Guide for Vendors Desiring to Contract for Business with Los Angeles County." It provides a wealth of insights as to how to go about lining up work. Your own county or nearby large city probably publishes similar guides.

Los Angeles County also holds a "Contracting Conference" every year. All departments are represented, and separate information tables are set up for the numerous contracting specialties, such as "custodial services." There may be similar conferences each year in your own area.

Large agencies also have purchasing departments with special desks for purchasing different commodities. You can obtain up-to-date lists of these items; they read like an index to the Yellow Pages, starting with "abrasives" and ending with "X-ray equipment." Here are some other resources from which to learn about moonlight opportunities:

- Local newspaper notices (under "Legal Notices" or "Bids Wanted")
- Bidder mailing lists on which you can be included (you will need to learn how to become an approved source)
- Posted notices of pending solicitations, usually found in the City Hall or in each department
- Government purchasing agents

If you're a serious player for government business, you must master the gobbledygook jargon, carefully adhere to the sometimes convoluted procedures, and meticulously follow instructions for proper documentation. Be prepared with whatever credentials may be needed, such as a specialty contractor's license.

Although some may suggest bidding low to get into the system, experienced vendors advise against this practice. It's better to take on a job you can manage successfully without cutting corners, and then develop a reputation for dependability.

Once started, you should deal directly with the staff, not the elected officials. For example, if you are performing work for a city and a council member calls up with a question or problem, keep the staff advised. The agency will want you to blend into their system, as if you were a servant of the citizens.

In some municipalities, contractors even use city business cards (since they are in fact agents of the city). This helps to foster the perception that you're an integral part of the city work force, because it makes the staff's job that much easier. In other words, melt into the structure. Let's assume a city has privatized its Parks Department. When the City Manager has a meeting with department heads, the contractor handling parks should be in attendance, shoulder-to-shoulder with the chief of police and other civil service management personnel. The more you can enhance this perception of being a part of the structure, the greater your chances will be of long-term relationships.

Under the system of RFPs, it's not merely price that determines who gets the contract when time comes around to re-bid; it's who gets along with others the best. If you have an employee embroiled in a personality conflict with someone on the staff, switch him or her to another job. Remember, the government can't easily fire an incompetent employee, but they can promptly terminate a contractor who is rubbing them the wrong way.

You will soon gain familiarity with the jargon and the procedures: the RFPs (requests for proposal) or the purchasing department's RFQs (requests for quotation). Each procedure has its own rules as to how contracts are to be let. The "MOU" (memorandum of understanding) can be a binding agreement as to the government's intentions, including which functions are to be privatized and which are not.

There is a cousin to privatization that should also be mentioned: performing services for private industries that in the past were normally handled in-plant. This is technically called "outsourcing" and is a result of the "hollowing" of corporate America (discussed in Chapter 12). For the same reasons that governmental bodies are privatizing, private business is doing likewise. Instead of depending on their own employees, firms struggling to cut costs are increasingly looking to outside contractors.

The garment industry's tradition in using independent contractors is now accepted protocol throughout American industry. No longer must companies restructure or file Chapter 11 in order to shed themselves of financially crippling labor contracts. The alternative is simply to subcontract the work. Your best prospects will be companies currently locked into high labor rates and fringe benefits that must break loose in order to survive.

As for local government services, I firmly believe that the time is ripe for privatization. Year after year, your local government faces increased service demands and inadequate revenues. Increasing taxes or cutting services is getting to be too politically risky. Aggressive contracting programs are one of the few realistic alternatives. You could find out very quickly just how receptive your local municipality is to "alternative service-delivery." By making inquiries you'll learn very fast whether there's a moonlighting play here.

If you're interested in more information about privatization in the form of articles, reports, and books, the country's leading source is the Local Government Center, a project of the Reason Foundation. LGC was formed to research all aspects of privatization and to make this information available to prospective contractors and local officials. Their services include a privatization database that includes a nationwide file listing which public services have been privatized by specific local governments across the country.

The Center also provides a computerized and regularly updated list of companies that provide public services, plus trade associations and privatization consultants. "Fiscal Watchdog," published by LGC, is the country's principal monthly newsletter reporting the latest on-going developments in privatization. Their address is: Local Government Center, 2716 Ocean Park Blvd., Suite 1062, Santa Monica, CA, 90405.

As a final update on the direction that privatization has taken, whatever do you think happened to Dan Heil? As you may remember, he was last reported working out of a trailer down in Dairy Valley. Today, Willdan Associates operates out of twelve regional offices, serves 250 governmental clients throughout the United States, and employs more than 350 professionals.

Heil is living proof of the view expressed by experts like the Reason Foundations's Robert Poole: "The fact today is that government is involved in hundreds, if not thousands of business activities in which it has no real comparative advantage and no basic reason for being involved." For moonlighters with smooth communication skills, privatization could become the next gold rush; like gold it's hard to mine, but once unearthed, extremely valuable.

PART FOUR   ▼   EASY DOES IT —
BUT DO IT

Here are some final practical tips for
moonlighters in any business.

—

# CHAPTER EIGHTEEN

# All in the Family

On television, entrepreneurs are generally not portrayed as admirable characters. More than likely, they're somewhat sleazy, standing alone (drink in hand) and stopping at nothing to accomplish their grubby goals. Less often, the entrepreneur is shown to be a champion of free enterprise, bravely fighting off the corporate rascals of the world. But in either characterization there's a common trait of sacrifice. Time for family and fun is set aside, and in its place endless hours are devoted to business.

This is *not* my idea of how you, the real-life moonlight entrepreneur, should go about starting a business. The overall measure of success will depend on how smoothly the sideline activity is woven into your life without disrupting your job or short-changing your family. The greatest dangers will be tripping over your job or ending up as a fatigued zombie.

You must keep firmly in mind that the purpose of moonlighting is to achieve something *better* for the future, something that will enhance rather than destroy what is most important to us all: our family ties. To succeed, you must abandon major portions of your domestic responsibilities. You're going to have to delegate. Learn the trick of multiplying your own time by enlisting the efforts of someone to function as your alter ego. When you're at the regular job, your counterpart will assume your role in the moonlight business.

As I've said, there are two solutions to the problem of time management: getting family members involved or taking on outside partners. In this chapter I will suggest how these alternatives can be brought into play. Of the two, "all in the family" is the most desirable choice for a number of reasons. Taking on an outside partner is also an option, but know that a number of conditions must be imposed in order to avoid jarring upsets. First let's look at some of the reasons why a family business is an ideal situation for moonlighting:

- ▶ Load sharing is easily arranged.
- ▶ Common goals pull the family together.
- ▶ You can utilize individual and collective family skills.

- Family members can work during hours you're on the regular job, which means you can opt for a business that is conducted during your own regular job hours.
- Conflict-of-interest accusations at work can be defused: "It's my *wife's* business!"
- Many find it to be a better solution to financial pressure than "working wives"; why not work as a team in the family business?
- The kids are given the means to earn pocket money in a controlled family environment.
- The kids are also taught the benefits of entrepreneurship.
- The business is set up with preestablished lines of authority and responsibility.
- The kids can take over the business later.
- Wives can enjoy an escape from household drudgeries and exercise their business capabilities.
- When all else fails (including your job), a family working together is the world's best survival unit.

An enterprise can work well with all sorts of relationships. Dick Rutan and Jeana Yeager were so dedicated in their mission as to have been like an "all in the family" unit during the two years of preparation leading up to their eight-day, round-the-world flight on Voyager. In your own case, your choice might be a business run by either your husband or wife who would assist you.

For example, a travel agency could be run by a nonworking wife during regular business hours, and the working husband could help out in his free time. An uncle could start a business that his nephews help run. It could be mother and son, brother and brother, or cousin and cousin.

Contrarily, it could be son and mother. I know one young man who started a moonlight flower business out of a rented stall in a shopping mall. He enlisted his mother and his aunt to do the selling during the hours he was at his own regular job. Obviously he could trust them in every conceivable way; he never had to worry about their not showing up or where the money went. Indeed, no one in the world was as anxious for his success as they were. His moonlight business grew so fast that it wore out both mother and aunt. But by then he was able to put together a team of employees to take over their roles.

A Los Angeles businessman had a son graduating from college who wanted to go to work for him. The father was in dress manufacturing and didn't want his son to have anything to do with it, because he felt it was such a schlocky business. So he started a moonlight business for the son to run, one in which the son had already gained experience during summer part-time jobs: making pizza. Dad became the financial angel, and everything else was left to the care of the junior entrepreneur. As it happened, the youngster did a terrific job of running the restaurant, and the business became enormously successful.

There can be as many possibilities as there are family members, and there are no hard and fast rules as to who should be boss. The organization chart can be carved out of a pecking order already in existence, and responsibilities can be divided in a hundred ways. It may be husband and wife as partners, each with complementing responsibilities. Perhaps the member of the household with the regular job won't be in charge at all, but backs up (if only in an advisory capacity) the front-line responsibilities of other family members. The following examples will give you a feel of how families can interact in moonlighting.

Lynn Boozer is a full-time elementary teacher who has successfully operated a moonlight business for the past twenty-two years. This has been made possible by a partnership with her twin sister, Barbara, who was also a full-time teacher until finally deciding to work at their business full time. They own a gold mine of a store called Frederick's Party Shop. Lynn's school days normally wind up at 2:35 P.M., and she then goes to the store two to three times a week as well as at night and some weekends.

"The Twins," as Lynn and Barbara are known in the trade, grew up listening to merchandising talk at the family dinner table. Their father worked for the S.H. Kress Company, and later went independent and operated five variety stores on his own. During their summer vacations the girls would work for their dad, learning the business from the bottom up. How much cozier could a family business be than twins learning the know-how from their father, and then following in the paternal footsteps!

Klara Bieber is a full-time real estate agent specializing in the sale of large homes. Her sales are in the seven-figure range every year, and she is forever on the go. Her husband is a computer engineer engaged in a moonlighting capacity by helping Klara at her work in many ways. On weekends it may be that she's involved in sitting at an open house. Her husband then helps out in all kinds of support activities: taking pictures of properties, preparing set-ups, helping cover the household responsibilities otherwise falling on Klara's already burdened shoulders, and every day lending support to her (very renumerative) efforts.

Judy Flores was a top escrow officer in a savings and loan association. Her interest in starting a business was fueled by three motives. First, she was yearning to scratch an entrepreneurial itch that wouldn't go away. She was also tired of real estate escrows (and tired of being downtown). Finally, her employer was falling on lean times, and she was fearful that the future of her job was shakey.

Since Judy was sick of her job, she decided that escrow work was the very *last* thing she wanted to do. (Otherwise it would have provided an excellent opportunity for an independent business.) Judy also wanted to follow her mother's example; for years she had worked out of her own home as a paralegal secretary for a number of Pasadena law firms.

While watching the "Two on the Town" TV show one evening, Judy was intrigued by a demonstration of a computerized typesetting machine. She discovered the computer had taken over the mechanical work traditionally done by typesetters. Sometimes spunky determination is kindled when opportunity collides with coincidence.

As it happened, Judy's husband Ron had been employed by a printing firm for twenty years and was well acquainted with the equipment demonstrated on the TV show. In fact, Ron's firm would frequently subcontract their overflow work to computer typesetters. With his employer's blessings, Judy and Ron started Penguin Typography Company in the guest bedroom of their condominium. Judy was the full-time entrepreneur and Ron was the part-time moonlighter.

Ron's familiarity with the printing industry obviously gave Judy an immediate advantage. Her start-up company already had twenty years of experience behind it when it began! Her first (and still biggest) customer is Ron's own employer, who subcontracts typesetting jobs to her that come in during overflow periods and which must be farmed out if they are to be completed on time.

Judy also took on subcontract work for five other printing firms, two of which are instant-print shops. While printers usually do their own typesetting, some are farming out this work so as to avoid not only the expensive labor but also prohibitively expensive investments in equipment. Judy says that it is not uncommon for this kind of business to be run by women, and that it's an appropriate activity for artistic people who have an eye for attractive page layout.

But this is an industry of rapid technological change. Desk-top computers and more sophisticated printers are rapidly replacing traditional typesetting in less demanding jobs such as newsletters. Judy is going to lose some business to desk-top printing; she must find other replacement business if she is to maintain her sales volume. She attributes her success to their mom-and-pop approach and especially to Ron's expertise. Judy doesn't think she could have done it without his help.

Alan Miller went into business for family reasons. He started the Original New York Seltzer line of sodas while he was still employed by TRW, the aerospace firm. His sales in 1987 were $100 million—from a business that was founded in 1982! Yet Miller worked as a developmental engineer for TRW until the summer of 1985, three years after starting his own company. He retired after his twentieth anniversary with the company. One reason he stayed so long with TRW was he felt that he might one day really need the pension. Now he doesn't.

He decided to revive a family seltzer business that had been inactive since the 1950s. Miller felt his son Randy "needed a career and I wanted to start a father-and-son business that we could both do on a daily basis." During the first three years of Original New York Seltzer, the going was hard. Alan, moonlighter to the core, lived a double life during this phase: one as founder of his new company, the other as full-time employee in his job.

Now that they're successful, Original New York Seltzer is bombarded by conglomerates that want to buy the company for huge sums of money. Miller says, "We started this business for Randy's career—so even if we don't see that kind of money, we won't sell. We're in the business for the long, long haul."

It's worth considering how such a spectacular family success story comes about. First of all, Alan Miller had his son's help in the early start-up days of the business. He could not have done it alone and therefore preserved his full-time career at TRW. It was only after the company was rolling that he quit his job. Also, the Miller family had a business heritage to start with; his grandfather in the early 1900s had sold (genuinely) "original" seltzer from a horse-drawn wagon in New York. In short, Alan and Randy knew how to do it, and they did it together.

Ann and Bill Kreile are now retired, but both were teachers and later administrators in the Los Angeles School District. During their careers, both engaged in an unusual moonlighting activity (we really can't call it a business) that substantially enhanced the pleasure of their retirement. In 1974 they put up $33,000 to purchase a residential lot located on a bluff in the seacoast town of Lucadia, California.

During a period of three years they prepared plans and then, acting together as owner-builder, tackled the job of building. They did it as a family. With the help of their children, casual labor, and hired trades, the Kreiles built a home and an apartment unit on the property. As construction moved along, they scraped up another $35,000 to pay the bills. The home was never intended to be their primary residence but was built as an investment.

Both home and apartment commanded a spectacular Pacific Ocean views and had direct access to the white, sandy beach below. The surge of inflation in the late 1970s caused the property to continue soaring in value, as did the limited supply of prime waterfront property. Finally, in 1985 Bill and Ann sold the property for $495,000. They're now enjoying a new Jaguar and if you were to try to call them, they would probably be out. My guess is they would be somewhere aboard the QE2. This moonlighting family has realized its dream.

Some entrepreneurs may be reluctant to inject the hard-nose aspects of running a business into their family life. There may also be communication and authority problems. I know that sometimes when Peggy consults me about her squeegee project, my advice is not always received with a smile. What is intended as a straightforward recommendation may sometimes appear as unacceptable bullying.

If something went berserk at Yum Yum, I was at liberty to bang heads or insist on corrective measures. While this attitude is possible in dealing with your children, it is decidedly not so easy to do with your wife, husband or parents. What it boils down to is that you can't talk to your wife with quite the same authority as you can to an employee.

So levels of authority must be carefully worked out when a moonlight business is brought into the household. It's like having a new baby; each parent's responsibilities had better be clear from the first. Who *is* the boss? Shall each of the partners have veto privileges?

A mom-and-pop business could produce the very frustration that you're trying to avoid in your job. One reason for moonlighting is to gain real authority, and in some mom-and-pop ventures this may be difficult to put into practice. Must both agree as to how thin the salami is to be sliced? Probably so.

In some instances, there may be other reasons that a mom-and-pop operation is not in the cards. Perhaps your family members are not available or interested, or possibly they are not possessed of enough entrepreneurial spirit to wish to be involved. You must then consider other possibilities. Going into moonlighting with a partner is the alternative, but there are some ghastly pitfalls for the unwary.

One such boobytrap is getting two families together in a business. More often than not, this results in all sorts of tensions. Too many players and too many claims to authority can result in a muddled operation. And clan loyalties operating at cross-purposes can produce a destabilizing effect rather than creating a business unit that has cohesive force.

Another possible difficulty with a partner is that we don't all operate at the same level of energy. This is bound to cause bad feelings. Sharon Van Tassel of Handy Helpers, whom you read about in Chapter 16, actually started out with a partner. Her business was an overnight success, but it soon became clear that she and her partner were not operating at the same level of dedication. It destroyed their relationship. Sharon found herself increasingly busy making the operation work, while her partner blissfully watched the new business roll in and took her 50 percent. The problem was finally resolved when Sharon took over the business 100 percent.

One of the reasons that my sixteen-year partnership with Frank Watase maintained stability was because both of us maintained a high degree of energy in running the business. The alliance would have been unworkable if I had always been out to lunch while Frank did the work, or vice versa. Instead, our mutually keen drives had a competitive aspect to them. If you moonlight with nonfamily partners, the following rules should be kept in mind:

- Be sure you're getting involved with someone with an equal level of energy—and a willingness to expend it.
- Be certain that your skills and experience complement one another. As William Wrigley put it, "When two men in business always agree, one of them is unnecessary."
- Have a buy/sell agreement in place before you embark, including a method (life insurance, perhaps) of funding a buy-out in the event of a partner's death.
- Incorporate the business. Otherwise if things go badly, you will become personally liable for the debts of your partner.

Let's examine some moonlight ventures started by outside-the-family partnerships. First, here's one that worked. Lu Hishmeh is an instructional advisor in the Los Angeles school system. She started her moonlighting career by following the principle of "find a need and fill it." Lu saw a serious deficiency in primary school children with limited English speaking skills who consequently had difficulty in learning math concepts explained in English.

Her idea was to design a bilingual set of math books to teach elementary students this specialized vocabulary. She didn't have the time to write the books, so she devised a plan to engage specially gifted teachers as partners to execute her idea. In this way she'd remain firmly in the driver's seat as editor yet delegate the grunt labor (in this case, writing) to others.

The publishing firm of Houghton Mifflin liked Lu's idea and gave her the go-ahead for seven booklets: one each for grades K through 6. She then assigned a teacher from each grade the job of defining the needs for that particular grade level, using a special format. While Lu had lots of backup assistance, she still retained a firm command of all editorial decisions. With this initial moonlight venture under her belt, she is now interested in furthering this sideline and expanding her role of managing editor of future educational books.

Melvin Barnes (not his real name) is an example of how a moonlighter can get into trouble by having a partner. His regular job is working as a real estate broker. And like so many others in this business, Melvin experiences cycles of glorious prosperity followed by wrenching dry spells. During one upswing of good times when he had some excess funds, he decided to break out of this roller coaster pattern by starting an unrelated moonlight business. His idea was to start something that would provide enough profit to maintain a steady cash flow, year to year.

Melvin didn't have any business in mind, nor did he have any relatives interested in joining him. But after searching the "business opportunity" columns of the Los Angeles *Times*, he finally came upon a man needing a financial partner for the importation of parrots from Mexico.

This business appealed to him because of the anticipated high return, and he wanted to get the most from his savings. At first glance it was not a high-risk project, so he jumped in, relying on the projections of his new partner.

Melvin's role in the business was to finance the construction of a quarantine station for the birds and to furnish necessary working capital. The first load of 180 parrots made it safely to the new station in Los Angeles, and Melvin proceeded to play bird-nursemaid for forty-five days. Then, the very day the parrots were to be cleared of quarantine (and sold off at enormous profit) the Department of Agriculture came to the conclusion that Melvin's partner had failed to secure adequate certification from Mexican and U.S. authorities. The entire batch of birds was confiscated, and Melvin ended up in foul territory as well: sans money, sans business, and almost sans his mind.

What started out as a sure thing ended up as a bitter and uniquely unprofitable episode in his life. In ninety days he had lost $45,000, all of his hard-earned savings. Obviously not all nonfamily partnerships run into this kind of difficulty; but when they do, the lessons are expensive ones. Melvin said afterwards that he'll never forget the following three rules about going into a moonlight partnership:

- ▸ Check out your partner very carefully.
- ▸ Never put up all of the required money; *both* partners should have something to lose if things go sour.
- ▸ Don't start out in reliance on someone else's knowledge if you cannot carry out the plan yourself. (Melvin knew nothing at all about importing exotic birds).

Some nonfamily relationships are so close as to be akin to family. This considerably broadens the definition of what we should consider to be "all in the family." Friendships can be like dealing with family because of long-term bonds that can be every bit as strong as blood ties. As Kipling puts it, "Thank God for a trusty chum!"

Doctors and lawyers, as well as other professionals, can also utilize the all-in-the-family approach to entrepreneurial ventures. Moonlighting in a business is a way for some professionals to satisfy a desire to experience freedom from the cloistered environment of, let us say, academia or medicine.

A physicist I met recently who teaches at New York University expressed a desire to do something that had a concrete, commercial purpose to it in order to complement his ethereal pursuits on the campus. Professionals can just as well stick to a moonlight business in their own field: physicians can operate clinics. Teachers can open trade schools or day-care facilities, hopefully with the help of others in the family.

Family members should consider enlisting their "in-house" professionals. If a husband practices law and his wife wants to start a business, their joint expertise could be pooled. The husband's legal background could provide help in not only setting up the venture but in managing ongoing business issues as well.

As it happens, I know a CPA who is a controller in a conglomerate, and whose wife is office manager for a doctor. These complementary credentials could result in all kinds of synergistic possibilities. For instance, her office skills could be utilized in managing a tax-consulting business.

You probably have observed how so many immigrants from the Far East earn their livings: they run businesses. And *everybody* in the family contributes; the kids clean the tables, grandma tends the stove, mother works the register, and dad waits on tables. The results are clear: these families are making astounding economic gains.

In southern California, almost all of the independent donut shops are run by Cambodians who have immigrated during the past ten years. Their success is not hampered by either a poor education or an inability to speak English. They operate without outside supervision, accounting, or administrative costs. They all just pitch in and work.

Another benefit of family moonlighting is that the business can re-unite families who have become dispersed through both parents working in jobs. A story in *Fortune* Magazine was entitled "Executive Guilt: Who's taking care of the children and how will they turn out?" The article was based on a survey of corporate women officials. "Quality time with children" was cited as the primary sacrifice they had made for their careers. And management psychologists agree that nothing tugs more at executive consciences than the fear of neglecting the kids during their most formative years.

According to Norman Lobsenz, in an article in the May 1988 issue of *Redbook*, the key to a family's strength and happiness is the degree of emotional closeness between members. Here are some of his suggestions as to how families can become closer:

- Make time to be together.
- Get to know one another.
- Share problems.
- Design a challenging family project.
- Share your work and school lives.

Now, aren't all of these ample reasons to think about a family business? Parents who can direct the children, even in a business, can escape the problems of splintered lives altogether. As Stanley Spiegel puts it, "What's most important is that the child is given a sense that he is a worthwhile human being." How better to accomplish this than to have the children not only at home but also joining in the family business? Americans at one time *did* work together, keeping shop or running the farm; it's just that in modern urban life we have forgotten how.

Keeping the venture in the family works because the entire support system is already set up and running. Members naturally work side by side, shoulder to shoulder, back to back. As in the Voyager, it took two to fly nonstop around the world; one rested while the other worked the controls. Moonlighting should not be approached as something done entirely solo. It will require others to cover for you when you're not at the controls.

My closing argument on behalf of bringing in the family is taken from no less an authority than King Solomon himself: "Two can accomplish more than twice as much as one. If one fails, the other pulls him up; but if a man falls when he is alone, he's in trouble. One standing alone can be attacked and defeated, but two can stand back-to-back and conquer; three is even better, for a triple-braided cord is not easily broken." And if the cord that binds is made of family strands, you can keep on the job and *know* that the moonlight business will be in good hands.

# CHAPTER NINETEEN

# It's Never Too Late

A seventy-five-year-old friend of mine, Robert Weil, was skiing at Mammoth Mountain last year with a friend, also seventy-five. As their chairlift drew near to the top of the mountain, and the magnificent view fully unfolded, Robert's friend experienced a moment of exaltation. He raised his hands to the heavens and exclaimed, "Oh, to be sixty again!"

It was Bismarck who established the age of sixty-five as that of retirement because in his day few Prussians lived that long. Now sixty-five is the prime of life. Life expectancy will soon be in the eighties, and prolonged vitality can be expected to accompany it. According to Dr. Walter Bortz II of Stanford Center of Medicine, many of the problems of aging are the consequence of not using our physical and mental equipment. He came to this conclusion after tearing an Achilles tendon; he was in a cast for six weeks. When the cast was removed, his thirty-five-year-old leg looked like the leg of a seventy-five-year-old: withered, stiff, and painful.

Yet involuntary idleness is increasingly the problem of older Americans. More than half of the firms on the *Fortune* list of the 1,000 largest U.S. corporations have undergone some form of significant reorganization entailing the drastic shedding of employees. Voluntarily or otherwise, the fifty-plus crowd is shifting from the ranks of the employed to the retired. This is coming about through normal (or early) retirement, being pushed out by younger competition, or even blanket firings of over-fifty employees resulting in people who no longer have jobs yet are too young to quit.

Many who retire in their fifties or sixties do not feel the absolute financial necessity of going back to work to make ends meet. Yet how can this growing retired population keep busy to avoid the sad fatigue of idleness? The automatic choice of most is to join the double and triple dippers: to return to work. However, the majority of private firms are not interested in hiring fifty-year-old start-ups. Instead, job opportunities for those over fifty are few and far between.

In 1920 there were fewer than five million people sixty-five or older in the entire United States; now there are more than twenty-five million. The UCLA Medical School projects that this population can be expected to double in the next thirty to forty years. No wonder, considering that deaths from heart disease, pneumonia and influenza (the leading causes of death in old age) have dropped 22 percent and 47 percent respectively. A wholesale change in how we eat and exercise and a decline in tobacco consumption has also led to a dramatic decline in deaths. In addition, ulcers, angina, and hypertension are all being brought under control.

All this is producing a blossoming contingent of retired, healthy Americans. We're now accustomed to the seventy-year-old student, the fifty-year-old retiree, and the sixty-five-year-old father of a preschooler. We find that healthy retired people are not by nature lazy, and even those who look forward to retirement are not looking so much to escape from work but from the tedium of their day-by-day job experience.

According to the Metropolitan Life Insurance Company, the average life span of those who have already reached sixty-five is eighty for men and eighty-four for women, which means that today those who leave regular careers at sixty-two or less are "retiring" at a decidedly awkward age. They are too young not to work yet too old to get new employment. We have created a society in which age is rapidly losing its relevance.

Those who retire are still free to work without the unrelenting demands of a full-time job. No longer must retirement conform to the traditional scenario of a farewell roast and a stressful move to Florida, followed up by vodka-embalmed idleness. Retirees now continue on with new careers—perhaps not the former nine-to-five routine, with greater emphasis on leisure activities.

When we leave a career, our occupation becomes "retired," a perfectly respectable status. Yet retirement should include some form of work; the answer lies in approaching retirement as a progression from career to ongoing productivity rather than a dead end. We only have a limited menu of choices:

▸ Do absolutely *nothing*.
▸ Engage in philanthropic activities.
▸ Go to work full or part time for another employer.
▸ Start a moonlight business.

The first alternative is simply unacceptable for anyone who wishes to maintain their vigor. Charitable work is for some an eminently productive and satisfying solution. I know of a retired executive who receives a full measure of satisfaction by following a simple daily routine. He wheels a cart of library books among the wards at the Childrens Hospital of Los Angeles. But not everyone can find fulfillment this way. The job market for retirees is simply too sparse to be a choice for most. Yet the final alternative, moonlighting on the side, offers some decidedly attractive advantages. Retirees already have:

- ▸ The capital
- ▸ The know-how
- ▸ The time

Retirees don't *need* to make big bucks (yet why shouldn't they make more?). Inactivity can be replaced by having fun with a business; the only conflict of interest may be the golf-starting time.

Perhaps the biggest objection to moonlighting after retirement is that making more than a certain amount of money can result in the loss of Social Security benefits. The rule is that if you're earning a living, you cannot at the same time collect Social Security. You may ask, "Why go the trouble of making money in a business if my Social Security check is reduced?"

If you are serious about moonlighting during retirement, there is a way out of this dilemma. You can incorporate the business and limit your salary to $6,000 per year until you reach sixty-five, and then $8,160 until you reach seventy, and not lose a penny in Social Security during those years. Earnings can stay in the business. Once you attain the age of seventy there will be no limits as to how much you can take out in salary without reduction in Social Security payments. Most businesses retain their earnings during start-up years anyway, to fuel growth.

The retired moonlighter should treat retirement as if it were now the primary job. It is, after all, a time to enjoy yourself. Moonlighting should enhance this time of life, not detract from its quality. The pleasure comes from being boss, being active, and accomplishing worthwhile objectives . . . for the fun of it.

Some examples will help you get the idea. Lou Flint is now fifty-five and has just ended a twenty-five-year career in computer programming. Yet even in this obviously sunrise field the unexpected can happen. His employer, Systems Development Corporation, was purchased by Burroughs Corporation. The consolidation turned into the usual game of musical chairs for the employees. And when the music stopped, Lou found himself without a job. Fortunately, he could readily get another one with his impressive programming credentials.

But in the meantime, to vent his desire to get away from the traditional routine, he embarked on the improbable temporary career of playing an "extra" on various TV series. His credits now include *Dallas*, *The Colbys*, *Hotel*, and the mini-series *War and Remembrance*. For years he didn't have a word to say about his work at the end of the day. Now his wife, Kathy, can't shut him up. As he says, "I've had more fun during these past weeks than I ever had at work over the past twenty-five years."

When you stop and think about it, Lou doesn't need to return to the jungle of corporate hassle and frustrating office politics. With his enhanced pension benefits, investments, and (later on) Social Security, he also has the option of retiring and becoming a moonlighter, either as a computer consultant or by pursuing his new career in TV. This could be engaged in as a controlled *sideline*, keeping firmly in mind that his main career would be "retired."

Nate Hurt spent thirty-five years with Goodyear. His last post was General Manager of Goodyear Atomic Corporation. But under the attack of Jimmie Goldsmith's hostile takeover efforts, things began to change fast. Goodyear was suddenly no longer a bastion of corporate bureaucracy. Crisis business decisions were made that in the past would have shattered the musty calm at headquarters. Among them was a deliberate build-up of horrific debts to mount a defense against the takeover. Goodyear's "planned restructuring" has resulted in greater efficiency, but at the expense of shedding entire divisions as well as thousands of employees. It was back to the basic business of rubber and tires.

Nate, along with many other top and middle managers, was offered early retirement. Here's a sixty-four-year-old executive at the prime of his productive life who was quite unexpectedly disengaged from his lifetime's work. He could have had a real problem with what to do with his life. It was not so much a matter of economic difficulty because he had achieved financial security through his enhanced Goodyear pension. His predicament was the sudden threat of growing—or feeling—old.

But there's no law that commits us to antiquity after reaching sixty-five. Nate had the good fortune to be offered another job with a firm he had previously done business with. The sudden threat of rusting solitude was solved by starting a new career, as he had done thirty-five years earlier as a young Goodyear trainee. This entailed moving from Akron to Albuquerque (not a bad idea in itself!), the construction of a new ranch home, and a completely fresh working environment.

Nate's wife Karen isn't ready to pass all her time playing bridge either. She decided to take on a new career as program director in an Albuquerque health care center. Both of their lives are made more interesting through activities than through the alternative of doing nothing at all. And supposing he didn't have the credentials to jump into a new job? His alternative could very well have been moonlighting on the side of the new full-time "job" of retirement.

Rudy Akre's career as a general maintenance man with National Dollar Stores lasted for twenty-five years. When he had to retire against his wishes (before he was emotionally ready for it) he simply went on doing as a moonlighter what he had been doing in his job. Over a period of years he built a circle of regular clients who called Rudy when ever things needed fixin'. Every morning someone would have a leaky faucet or an electrical circuit that didn't work. He was not only doing what he loved to do but was also his own boss, operating out of his home.

He never made a lot of money, because he never cared to charge much. But that didn't matter. It was a long, happy and completely fulfilling period of his life. Rudy performed this moonlight work for fifteen years until the age of eighty when his eyesight finally gave out, and he was forced into real retirement. And without that daily contact with the outside world, like the leg in the cast, he began to go downhill fast.

I will concede that some have no desire to work after retirement. For these folks, retirement brings a welcome end to drudgery and a new freedom to travel and do the things that were always denied them by the pressure of work. Travel tours are packed with those who go about retirement as an act of earnest revenge against their years of unwilling toil. Going back to work is the last thing on their minds; they're perfectly happy to do nothing at all. Whether literal retirement is better than staying productive is a personal matter. But if we follow the advice of the gerontologists, the best prescription is to stay active in some form of useful activity.

I know a naval officer who retired "at twenty" when he was forty years old and who has been doing *zilch* for the past fifteen years. From his point of view, why shouldn't he? His government pension is indexed to inflation, and in a modest way he can get by. And to be honest, during occasional intervals of weariness I sometimes secretly envy him—until I drive through towns such as Hemet, Yucca Valley, or Fort Lauderdale, where having nothing to do is apparently mandated by city charter. But it's my guess that even in these snoozing communities there are hidden pockets of retired moonlighters, like Snow White's little friends, whistling away at their work.

My former next-door neighbor, a retired tycoon, died recently at the age of eighty-four. He had been retired for fifteen years, yet he stayed active in business and golf to the end. He relished every minute, except for that final year blighted by terminal illness. His surviving wife, on the other hand, doesn't even leave her house. Her life is in a self-perpetuated cast.

Yet Mary Smith, a pioneer real estate broker in Hollywood, California, worked full time until her death at the age of ninety-one. She managed the office of her son Patrick Smith, who is my commercial real estate broker. Until the very end, Mary enjoyed one (or two) Canadian Club Manhattans with her lunch. Her work kept her bright as a penny and very happy.

I can cite instances of productive retirement all day long. A school administrator became a political lobbyist. One couple does nothing more than creating dried flower arrangements and selling them to boutiques. A retired mechanic put up a shingle reading "Cadillac Specialist, forty-five years experience." A couple in their seventies retired from real estate brokerage and decided to build fourteen condominiums rather than simply sell off the property they owned. (They ended up making a fortune.) Then there are the retired cement foremen of the world like Rosario Jiminez who become general contractors.

Rosario is now *numero uno* in the pecking order every day. At the same time he's providing employment for his sons and nephews and heaven knows how many others. When you think about it, what is there to lose by moonlighting during retirement? You're no longer scrimping for the kid's education, keeping up with the neighbors, or serving time in a job. Why *shouldn't* you create some waves?

It's normally mom and pop who put the kids into business. But the reverse can also happen: the kids can put the retired folks into business. I happen to know the mother and father, both eighty-four, of a middle-aged professional woman. Both parents were turning into vegetables. With a little money down, the daughter bought a six-unit apartment building in the retirement town of Desert Hot Springs. Her folks now live in one of the units and manage the others. Suddenly they have a purpose to their lives, and both have shed the numbing effects of years of apathy. They're no longer a financial drain on the daughter and are happier to boot.

Happiness for the retired is normally not a matter of gaining more worldly possessions. By the 1980's, it was clearly established that mental attitude can be a lifesaver. *Newsweek* magazine of October 20, 1986, in a feature article entitled "Why We Age Differently," stated that scientists had begun to suspect that decline is not an inevitable consequence of aging. Supporting this belief, the Human Population Laboratory at Berkeley determined after a twenty-year study that people who are socially isolated had a much higher risk of illness and death than people with friends and family. And according to gerontologist Dr. James Fries of Stanford University, we are moving toward a more "rectangular" lifespan, in which we'll enjoy prolonged health followed by a relatively short drop-off into illness and death.

There is overwhelming data to demonstrate that activity promotes longevity. Skylab astronauts, who are weightless and physically inactive in space, lost so much calcium from their bones that scientists concluded that long space flights would be crippling. Sedentary people develop problems with heart functions; they also lose body mass and red blood cells. Whether aged or not, an inactive body develops most, if not all, the negative aspects associated with old age.

Research has also shown that not even memory necessarily decreases with age. The National Institute on Aging concluded that old people in excellent health have memories just as sharp as those in their twenties. The research tested memory in sixty men aged twenty to eighty-five and found no age-associated difference in verbal memory (such as remembering appointments or what people said to them). These findings coincided with what Edward Schneider of USC's Andrus Gerontology Center concluded:

"There is no evidence that aging causes any impairment of intelligence or ability to make decisions."

No age group commands the same financial resources as the retired generation. In fact, 77 percent of all individual financial holdings are in the hands of the fifty-plus age-group. According to the Federal Reserve Board, the assets of the fifty-five-year-old-and-up head of household average more than $50,000 while in the corresponding thirty-five to fifty-year-old group, assets total about $18,000 on the average. In recent years the older population has also begun to spend more of its income than in previous years. Retired people as a class are impressively affluent, more so certainly than younger aspirants who are still scrimping, still saving, and still paying off debts.

There are two more moonlighting advantages that the retired have over the young: the experience of already having made their business mistakes and (hopefully) the wisdom gained by learning from them. In Japan, workers often begin entirely new careers after retirement because the Japanese have an inherent reverence for the experience that age provides. This wisdom gained from maturity dovetails perfectly with the model of structured prudence required of moonlighters.

You might say that retirement is not a period of life during which you should put the family jewels at risk in a business. I quite agree. The *last* thing the retired moonlighter needs to do is to put more at risk than can be safely lost. But remember that the rule of Chapter 8, "Limit your Liability," applies just as emphatically to the retired as to any one else.

For many retirees, working for someone else would be simple therapy, but not many can easily slip into jobs. But starting a business is quite different; it's not the exclusive territory of the young. In fact, quite the opposite is true. Starting-up is more important to the retired than it ever was for the young having no choice in the matter. For the retired, work becomes the candy of life, no longer fueled by the imperatives of putting bread on the table, raising the kids, or paying off the mortgage. "I owe, I owe, it's off to work I go!" is not the tune the retired moonlighter hums.

Moonlighting in a business can be nothing less than preventative therapy against a degrading decline into extinction. You can work for yourself—and be boss at last! Like love, it's simply too good to be wasted entirely on the young.

# CHAPTER TWENTY

# Moonlighters, Start Your Engines!

Nearly six million Americans now hold down two jobs. Americans actually want to work *more* rather than less, a commitment far stronger than previously imagined. Could this be setting the stage for a blossoming of entrepreneurship in the United States? At the present, only an elite clan are running our businesses. But the new wave of immigrant entrepreneurs are now giving courage to millions of Americans who in the past were satisfied to work in jobs—and even in second jobs.

We see this new wave of entrepreneurs when we go to the market, the cleaners, or the gas station. Slowly we are waking up to the fact that running a business is no longer the preference of the uncommon few but can instead become the choice of the working population as a whole. As entrepreneurship becomes more visibly attractive, it also becomes part of the public domain.

In Hong Kong this has already happened. The influx of Chinese refugees in the late 1940s went to work in businesses, resulting in the entire colony suddenly emerging into an entrepreneurial—and incredibly rich—way of life. It could be the same way here.

For many, the spirit may be willing, but deciding on which business to engage in can turn into a frustrating deadlock. To help you decide, I suggest that you blend together some of the subjects covered in previous chapters to see if a recipe suitable for your own situation emerges. Let's start by listing some of the available ingredients:

The single-product solution    All in the family

The hollow corporation    ·Serving people

Real estate    Direct marketing

Privatization    Our daily bread

Each of these represents a possibility for moonlighting. But any of them standing alone is less potent than two or more together. So why not combine two or more of them? One plus one may add up to more than two, and you may come up with a bull's eye idea.

For example, let's say that you're very good at making chili. Already you have a couple of advantages going for you: "our daily bread" and "single-product solution." We will also assume that your spouse is willing to do the cooking (all in the family). Given all this, you already have the perfect combination for a moonlight venture.

Let's combine three other subjects we have covered in this book: "real estate," "hollow corporation," and "serving people." The resulting business could be to develop self-storage lockers on low-cost land that will appreciate in value over the years. You could also subcontract the building of a speculative house or develop small shopping centers. Do whatever you think is best given your own skills and circumstances.

How about combining "direct marketing," "our daily bread," and "hollow corporation"? This could translate into the sale of your own private-label food product. A detailed explanation shouldn't be necessary to show how moonlighting opportunities can surface when you blend winning traits together. You can develop your own list of combinable traits in order to come up with a moonlighting opportunity that is tailor-made for you.

Surely the main objective is to get into a business you will enjoy. You can then couple this activity with other, equally favorable ones. Let's assume that you and your spouse enjoy traveling to New England in the fall. Perhaps the two of you, operating as "mom and pop," could build a specialty business of promoting and conducting "The Inns of New England Adventure" tours (a "single-product solution").

Once you have decided on your moonlight business, there is finally another essential ingredient: down-to-earth staying power. The hard-nosed entrepreneur has the dedication to plow through hardships to success. Orson Welles was a genius, and he produced at least one true masterpiece. But his drive for artistic perfection got in the way of completing his film projects within budget and on time. He simply did not possess the determination to keep a tight rein on the economic aspects of his ventures. Welles' aesthetic approach got in the way of his success as an entertainment entrepreneur.

Panhandle Eastern Corporation ran a series of advertisements that cited staff conversations with people widely recognized as perennial leaders in their professions. Panhandle Eastern hoped to provide insight into the enduring values and attitudes that lead to success over a long period. One such talk was with Joe Paterno, the legendary football coach at Penn State, who has compiled one of the best records in football while emphasizing academic excellence.

Now, Joe Paterno happens to be the greatest authority on staying power I know. I firmly believe that the qualities needed to win at sports are the same as those required for success in business. Here are some of

Joe Paterno's ideas on winning at football, which you can apply to your own moonlighting venture:

▶ Having a bad start was probably the best thing that ever happened to me . . . now I constantly question everything I do.
▶ If you're knocked down you can't lose your guts. You need to play with supreme confidence or else you'll lose again, and then losing becomes a habit.
▶ You must always do what you're afraid to do. People aren't just lucky. Good things happen to them because they're willing to take chances.
▶ If you don't win, you don't win, but at least you have the experience of going for it.
▶ Some players think that when Saturday comes, they can get by on natural ability, that practice isn't important. That's foolish. In our league, everyone is good. If you want to be #1, you better get yourself ready.
▶ The will to win is important, but the will to prepare is vital. Our players work so hard in practice, Saturdays seem easy by comparison.
▶ You don't know what you have until you have to use it.

Before you embark on your moonlight journey, your entrepreneurial engine must be properly tuned. Here's a diligence checklist to insure that you are ready. The purpose of such a methodical approach is to uncover any area of unpreparedness. For instance, you may have selected a great business, but you had better make certain it is suitable for moonlighting as well. Then when the wheels do hit the road, you won't find yourself careening out of control because you're unable to handle both job and business.

1. First of all, are you in the right job? Your job is the basic foundation. Decide carefully whether you should continue if you have significant forebodings.
2. Do you believe in the moonlighter's basic game plan of not quitting your job? If your moonlight endeavor blossoms to make your job redundant, then at some future time you can decide whether to quit—not when you're starting out.
3. If you traded places with your employer, how would you as the employer look upon the moonlight venture your employee is about to begin? Self-interest and enthusiasm can override good judgment about conflicts of interest. If you're unsure, pass the dice.
4. Have you carefully picked the right business? You only have so much time for your laps around the track. Pick a business you enjoy and feel lucky in: one that puts a gleam in your eye. And keep in mind

that the best drivers have close emotional attachments to their vehicles, whether cars, planes, or businesses.

5.  This item is not a question but a statement. The moonlight entrepreneur is not a full-throttle risk taker. By following the rules to "Limit Your Liability," you can become a player without risking everything.

6.  Have you learned accounting? It's a lot more fun (and safer) playing when you know the score. It's also cheaper, since you don't need to hire outsiders. Leave it to the accountants to audit your work and prepare your tax returns. (Nobody is going to learn *that* trick in school.)

7.  Have you planned cash flow for the first year? To complete the race you need enough gas in the tank. Hard cash is your business fuel, and cash-flow planning is the method to inform you how much you'll need. You can then forge ahead with assurance, knowing from the outset that cash has been adequately provided for.

8.  This item is not a question or statement, but a plea. Work for someone else in the business before starting out. If necessary, mop the floors. If possible, do a bit of everything. You'll learn operating tricks that will verify your beliefs, blow up your mistaken concepts, and grant you the self-confidence to start up your own engine.

9.  Is it possible to first prove your concept in a pilot operation? In the laboratory of trial and error, mistakes can be corrected. Glitches can be un-glitched. Miscalculations are not always so easy to deal with when everything you have decided to risk is at stake.

10. Can you narrow your focus to the "single product solution"? I must constantly remind myself of the "KISS" doctrine: Keep It Simple, Stupid. It works beautifully for moonlighters. How can you fail if all of your energy is concentrated on a single product?

11. Can your moonlight business be hollowed? There are abundant reasons to contract out your work. For one thing, you probably can find someone to manufacture your product more cheaply than you can make it yourself. And you won't have a dime invested in equipment, plant, or (worse still) labor.

12. How about keeping it "all in the family"? For moonlighting, such an approach is a round peg for a round hole. Or, if not in the family, start up with a trusted friend. Share the work load and benefit from the strength of complementary talents.

13. Are you quite sure you're not going into the marketplace with a product that someone in Seoul or São Paulo won't be able to blow out of the water? If you're unable to negotiate rock-bottom prices in your own home town, look to other (worldwide) vendors. In other words, if you can't beat 'em, join 'em!

14. As described earlier in this chapter, how about cooking up a moonlight recipe by combining traits already been proven to be successful? Write them down on separate cards and see what winning hands you can shuffle up for yourself. Working out this puzzle can become an amusing obsession, but the stakes are far-reaching. An ounce of shrewd selectivity at the outset will be immensely appreciated later on. The wrong choice could put you in a swamp—and up to your neck in alligators—for years to come.

15. Are you willing to share the fruits of your success with those who help make it come true? The original Three Musketeers Bar was shaped to be broken easily into three roughly equal pieces. The sales slogan was "Big enough to share with a friend!" Today it's a single piece with no suggestion of division. Their advertising campaign now depicts a young boy hiding in his closet, eating his candy far away from other people who might enjoy sharing it. This doesn't work in business; you must motivate those who are pulling at the oars. And the best way to do this is by generous profit incentives.

Here are two closing reminders. As a moonlighter you cannot tolerate unproductive labor. If you can subcontract, all the better for you. By doing so, you won't become a victim of the surging waves of change in the labor market and the increasing mandates for employer-paid fringe benefits. Also, I urge you again to become an expert in your business before starting out. It is difficult for most entrepreneurs to take this precaution. After deciding which business to start, work for someone else in that line of business first, learning everything there is to know. *Then, and only then,* start your engine, because once you are committed to the race, you will be driving head-to-head against experienced professionals who give no quarter to amateurs.

I have a friend who is interested in starting an auto paint shop as a moonlight operation. He has learned through a business seminar that this field has become "hollowed"; the labor is now subcontracted on a piecework basis, including the commission selling, the body and fender work, and the painting. He is willing to throw his hard-earned savings into this venture because of the rosy figures appearing in a pro forma profit-and-loss statement.

Yet he remains stubbornly unwilling to work in the business to find out what the race is all about. He has no idea what pitfalls lie ahead and doesn't want to go to the trouble of walking the track before he starts his engine. Instead he hopes to induce a fellow who works in the service department of a car dealership to be his manager.

My friend doesn't feel it's necessary to get his hands dirty because his manager will know everything. As foolish as this approach may seem, believe me, it's done all the time. Only after it's too late do such people wake up to realize that they're in a race they cannot win.

Is it possible that the demands of some careers could make moonlighting unwise? In certain instances, the answer is yes. You could face long hours or unusual responsibilities that do not leave sufficient time for family duties, let alone business. If this is so, your job probably offers enough of a challenge to make moonlighting redundant.

I have already mentioned the young fellow earning a great deal of money by working in the sound department of a major motion picture studio. As much as his entrepreneurial instincts leave him yearning for a business of his own, he has the good sense to realize that it would not be prudent to risk losing his lucrative job by moonlighting. His long and irregular hours at work simply don't leave him the necessary time.

We all are free to try out the entrepreneurial life. As a moonlight entrepreneur, you will achieve a degree of self-actualization very few working Americans ever experience. You'll enjoy unshackled liberty from the fiefdoms, the politics, and the pecking orders of a job. As Katherine Jensen puts it, "Life is like bein' on a mule team. Unless you're the lead mule, all the scenery looks about the same."

We may be the land of the free but we are decidedly not the home of the brave, because most Americans spend forty years obediently tolerating the boss. Many will talk big, but that's it. Others may secretly yearn for escape or even plan for it, but most are dissuaded by discouraging advice from the grandstand.

But remember that while the expression "more guts than brains" may adequately describe the full-time entrepreneur, it's *not* the nature of the successful moonlighter. Guts can propel one into taking silly risks, but the moonlighter isn't even going to quit the nine-to-five job! The essence of moonlighting is discipline, not mindless guts.

Prudent, dedicated moonlighters can accomplish their objectives. And if you're a true moonlighter, an entire chorus of discouraging advice won't keep you from your mission. Nor will setbacks get in your way. Our piece is said best for us by Walter Lippman: "I have never cared for an upholstered life, and, please God, I never shall. The protected existence, as I see it, is to refuse the risks, to be acquiescent, to sit tight. . . . "

A protected existence is not satisfying enough for the moonlight entrepreneur. In spite of our job-dependency, our sweaty-palmed fear of failure, and a deafening chorus of distractors, we are going to take that jump into the unknown. And when we start the engine, we will be prepared. In time, this exciting adventure will lead to the realization of our dreams.

# INDEX